Real Deceptions

Real Deceptions
The Contemporary Reinvention of Realism

Jennifer Friedlander

Oxford University Press is a department of the University of Oxford. It furthers the University's objective of excellence in research, scholarship, and education by publishing worldwide. Oxford is a registered trade mark of Oxford University Press in the UK and certain other countries.

Published in the United States of America by Oxford University Press
198 Madison Avenue, New York, NY 10016, United States of America.

© Oxford University Press 2017

All rights reserved. No part of this publication may be reproduced, stored in a retrieval system, or transmitted, in any form or by any means, without the prior permission in writing of Oxford University Press, or as expressly permitted by law, by license, or under terms agreed with the appropriate reproduction rights organization. Inquiries concerning reproduction outside the scope of the above should be sent to the Rights Department, Oxford University Press, at the address above.

You must not circulate this work in any other form
and you must impose this same condition on any acquirer.

Library of Congress Cataloging-in-Publication Data
Names: Friedlander, Jennifer, author.
Title: Real deceptions : the contemporary reinvention of realism / Jennifer Friedlander.
Description: New York : Oxford University Press, [2017]
Identifiers: LCCN 2016055980 | ISBN 9780190676131 (pbk) |
ISBN 9780190676124 (cloth) | ISBN 9780190676162 (Oxford scholarship online)
Subjects: LCSH: Aesthetics. | Realism in art—Philosophy. |
Art—Political aspects. | Feminist theory.
Classification: LCC N70 .F755 2017 | DDC 701/.17—dc23
LC record available at https://lccn.loc.gov/2016055980

To Falafel Jones (1950–2016) forever with love: in honor of your search for how to properly arrive at truth.

CONTENTS

Acknowledgments   ix

Introduction: Realism and Deception   *1*
1. The Realistically Deceptive, or the Deceptively Real? Ron Mueck and the Internal Illusion   *17*
2. Documentary Real-ism: *Catfish* and *This Is Not a Film*   *31*
3. An Uncertain Indeterminacy: Aliza Shvarts's Unseen Senior Project   *51*
4. A Ruse for the Real: Christoph Schlingensief's Deportation Installation   *59*
5. The Faux and the *Schmo:* Parodying Reality TV   *67*
6. Corporeal Realism: *Bodyworlds* and *Cloaca*   *79*
7. "Something I Can't Quite Articulate": Breastfeeding and the Real   *91*
8. *Melancholia* and the Real of the Illusion   *111*
Conclusion: On Being Duped   *123*

Notes   131
Bibliography   145
Index   151

ACKNOWLEDGMENTS

I have been enormously fortunate to have had the unconditional support of many people I love throughout the long process of writing this book.

Thank you to brilliant friends and colleagues who have sustained me over the years through innumerable acts of kindness, especially Mark Andrejevic, Stephanie Harves, Rachel Lindheim, Genna Miller, Carol Ockman, Mary Paster, Frances Pohl, Vin de Silva, Sean Spellman, Zala Volcic, Peggy Waller, Gary Wilder, and Meg Worley.

Much of the writing of this book has taken place in Vienna, and would have been impossible if not fueled by the tremendous encouragement, good cheer (and many, many spritzers) provided by dear friends: Klemens Brugner, Franziska Eberhart, Inaki Ezpeleta, Dagmar Serfezi, Otchie Stranzinger, Wolfgang Strazinger, and Carmen Visus. The gorgeous food, décor, and hospitality (not to mention the eternally replenished Wienerwasser) offered by Café Corbaci made it such a pleasure to sit and write each summer. Thank you, too, to my Melbourne "offices," especially Jimmy Watson's and DOC Espresso for never seeming to mind how long I lingered.

I am deeply fortunate to have cherished friends who are also intellectual comrades: Justin Clemens, Russell Grigg, Hilary Neroni, Todd McGowan, Robert Pfaller, and Michaela Wünsch. Their brilliance and unstinting generosity make possible previously unimaginable ways of thinking and being.

Thank you to Kevin Song for his tireless assistance, and for always asking what more he can do after already doing everything.

I am enormously grateful to Norm Hirschy for his enthusiastic and expert handling of the manuscript.

My life has been indescribably enriched due to the unstinting encouragement and generosity of my wonderful family. My exceptional parents, Mark Friedlander and Marybeth Friedlander, have given me the gift of unqualified love and the consequent courage to follow through on my desire. My wildly talented aunt, Vicki Iorio, and my extraordinary grandmother, Roslyn Vener, are strong and remarkable women who have had an incredible impact on me. I am so fortunate to be surrounded by so many other radiant and creative spirits that populate my family: Karen Iorio Adelson, Henry Wagons, Melvis Crawford, and Casper Wagons.

And to my supreme loves, who have nurtured me so tenderly through the ontological insecurities of writing this book: Josef Krips, whose affection and humor makes me forget everything else and continually teaches me the joys to be had in entering into fiction; and Henry Krips, whose luminous wisdom is as welcoming as it is deep, is the only one with whom I want to enter the impossible.

Finally, I would like to thank publishers for allowing me to use material that has appeared in earlier forms. I include the citations here:

"No Business like *Schmo* Business: Reality TV and the Fetishistic Inversion." *International Journal of Žižek Studies* 1, no 1.3 (2007):1–17.

"Representing Uncertainty/Claiming Indeterminacy: Aliza Shvarts' Unseen Yale Art Project." In *Resolutions3: Global Networks of Video*, edited by Ming-Yuen Ma and Erika Suderburg, 235–240. Minneapolis: University of Minnesota Press, 2012.

"Imperfecting the Illusion: Belief and the Aesthetic Destruction of Reality." *Discourse: Journal for Theoretical Studies in Media and Culture* 35.3, Fall (2013): 384–399.

"Public Art and Radical Democracy: Christoph Schlingensief's Deportation Installation." In *Urbanity. The Discreet Symptoms of Privatization and the Loss of Urbanity*, edited by content associates, 11–19. Vienna: Palgrave MacMillan, 2013.

"Breast Feeding and Middle-Class Privilege: A Psychoanalytic Analysis of 'Breast is Best.'" *Subjectivity* 8, no. 1 (2015), 74–91.

"Documentary REAL-ism: A Lacanian approach to 'This is Not a Film' and 'Catfish.'" *CiNéMAS: Journal of Film Studies*. Issue: *Revoir Lacan*, vol. 26, no 1, 2016. pp. 69–91.

"How to Face Nothing: *Melancholia* and the Feminine." In *Lars von Trier's Women*, edited by Rex Butler and David Denny, 201–214. New York: Bloomsbury Press, 2017.

"Corporeal Difference: *Body Worlds* and *Cloaca*." In *theory@buffalo* 19 issue, "Difference: Sexual, Cultural, Universal." January, 2017.

Real Deceptions

Introduction

Realism and Deception

During a family trip to Manhattan, we enticed our then three-year-old son, Josef, to go with us on an evening stroll by promising him that we could visit the animal sculptures he had spied earlier outside an art shop a few blocks away from our hotel. When we discovered that the bronzed animals had been locked inside for the night, we attempted to forestall what seemed like an inevitable meltdown by assuring Josef that if he stayed calm and kept walking, we were certain to encounter something equally special. And there, on the very next block, stood an incarnation of every three-year-old's idol: Elmo. With a combination of awe and apprehension, Josef walked up to Elmo and gave a tentative wave. Elmo, to my initial horror, responded with a polite but disinterested "Hi. How are you?" in a deep voice that made no attempt whatsoever to mimic Elmo's high falsetto. Upon hearing this surprising voice, Josef looked at me with what I first mistook for fear, but turned out to be elation: "Mommy, it's the REAL Elmo!" he exclaimed.

What was it that made Elmo seem real? Was it simply his presence in the fur—as it were—rather than as a two-dimensional image on the glowy box? Or could it be that somehow "Elmo's" very *infidelity* to the fiction lent him a more realistic status? Rather than prop up the illusion that Elmo is "real," this 47th Street Elmo revealed the truth, namely that Elmo is a fictitious character, who is often embodied and/or voiced by "real" folks—in this case by a man trying to earn a living in the heat of the New York summer by dressing in a heavy fur-coated suit and posing for pictures with preschoolers at a dollar a snap.

What might we glean from this encounter regarding the relationship between realism and deception, and how, if at all, might the interaction between realism and deception be used to facilitate an aesthetic politics? By taking up the overt trappings of Elmo, while simultaneously refusing to commit to the fiction that he was Elmo, the costumed man disturbed our expectations regarding the maintenance of a gap between fiction and reality. Our Elmo revealed the deception that is usually masked in carrying out the realist illusion. Such a revelation creates in viewers the "curiosity, the desire to see closer up," *but*—and this is the key point—the hope of reaching a final truth through a nearer view is always dashed.[1] Encounters with representations that invite the viewer to peek at the reality behind the artifice perpetuate the fantasy that there is a reality behind the fiction (even if it is one that we did not expect to find) rather than confront us with the more disturbing recognition that there might indeed be nothing behind the fiction.

Jacques Rancière's conceptualization of aesthetic politics, with which this book closely engages, requires us to abandon the idea that the disruptive potential of realism emerges from its ability to reveal a truth that has been masked by a deceptive appearance. Rather than think vertically in terms of "surface and substratum," he is committed to "think[ing] in terms of horizontal distributions, combinations between systems of possibilities."[2] To be specific, for Rancière, the possibility of equality without hierarchy is thwarted by the process of seeking to uncover a masked truth: "where one searches for the hidden beneath the apparent, a position of mastery is established."[3] By not taking the fiction seriously, Elmo stages a different deception, which might also facilitate such a position of mastery: he creates the illusion that if one can do away with fiction, one can arrive at the truth. This book will argue to the contrary that, in Jacques Lacan's terms, it is only by committing to the fiction that one can encounter truth.

An engagement with this Lacanian premise in conjunction with Rancière's conception of "aesthetic politics" will inform the analyses in the chapters that follow. As a preliminary, we consider an inverse of the Elmo case via an engagement with a politically incorrect television commercial for the Australian beer Toohey's. As we will see, in this scenario, rather than surprise the viewer by abandoning the fiction, the central figure takes the fiction too seriously. The ad opens with a man walking a small dog; he passes a pub from which an attractive woman sitting by the window beckons him to come and join her. He begins to enter the pub but pauses when he sees a "No dogs allowed" sign. The next shot reveals the man, now wearing dark glasses, entering the pub with his dog. The bartender quickly tells him that there are no dogs allowed. With a subtle but confident nod downward, the man says, "Guide dog," as he determinedly makes his way inside. The bartender, in no way fooled by this ridiculous attempt at dissimulation says, "Sorry mate, guide dogs are Labradors or German shepherds." Without missing a beat our protagonist says in mock horror, "What have they given me?"

By contrast with "Elmo," who distanced himself from the ostensible fiction, here we are faced with a character who commits too fully to a ridiculous fiction. When it is clear that his farcical deception has been unsuccessful—indeed, it could never have even been seen as more than a joke in the first place—the prankster surprises us by inhabiting the fiction even more deeply rather than giving it up. This performance flirts with the Lacanian structure in which, by committing to the fiction, one can arrive at truth, but, I contend, it falls short.

An explanation for its failure helps set the scene for what is involved in the development of an aesthetic politics that takes deception as the lure to the truth. The deception which the Toohey's prankster practices exceeds the fiction of possible reality and becomes a straightforward mockery. In this sense, like "Elmo's" enticement to "see through" the fiction to the hidden reality, the prankster's excessive devotion to the ruse invites viewers (diegetic and nondiegetic alike) to inhabit the position of mastery—of being securely "in the know." Although both of these examples play with structures that might facilitate disruptive encounters, each proves inadequate, but for different reasons.

To be specific, both "Elmo" and the dog owner entice the spectator to commit what Slavoj Žižek refers to as "the error of the existence of metalanguage, the illusion that, while taking part in illusion, one is somehow also able to observe the process from an 'objective' distance."[4] But the two examples prop up this illusion in inverse ways. In the Elmo encounter, the gap between the act of enunciation and the enunciated content is widened. By highlighting the incongruity between them, the costumed man unsettled the illusion of their predictable, harmonious, and inconspicuous relationship. This example then would seem to carry the disruptive potential that Rancière locates in moments in which "the eye does not know in advance what it sees and thought does not know what it should make of it."[5] Such moments challenge the taken-for-granted sensible schema in which hierarchies of perception are implicitly maintained. In particular, by calling attention to the ways in which the enunciation is always imbricated with the enunciated, "Elmo" may be seen to have compromised the illusion that metalanguage objectively grounds speech. But, I contend, rather than facilitating a disturbing recognition of the impossibility of metalanguage, this example demonstrates the way in which the illumination of the gap between the act of enunciation and the enunciated content may work in the opposite direction: the palpable mismatch between the form of enunciation and the enunciated content is smoothly realigned once recognized as an artifact of a hypercommercialist environment and socioeconomic circumstances. "Elmo," like so many, was merely (and barely) "going through the motions" of his job. But rather than undermine the grip of the ideological fantasy, not taking his role seriously works to uphold its power. As Žižek points out, ideology is not compromised by, but rather *depends upon*, subjects' ability to distance themselves from it.

Not taking one's role seriously is what "makes an ideology 'workable.'"[6] As he famously puts it: "even if we do not take things seriously, even if we keep an ironical distance, *we are still doing them*."[7] Here we see that the ready availability of a conventionally "political" explanation points to the very "apolitical" (in Rancière's sense) nature of the event. Such a conventional account of the political, in which an appearance gives way to the truth of socioeconomic relations, secures the impression of the existence of metalanguage as an objective, external position from which truth and falsity can be adjudicated. But, for Rancière, an aesthetic politics does not involve representations which seek to make a viewer aware of sociopolitical injustice and to mobilize in opposition to them. Rather, for Rancière, an aesthetic politics is achieved when new forms of visibility interrupt expected coordinates for making sense of an injustice rather than simply opposing it. In other words, such interventions must challenge the conditions of intelligibility. One of the ways for this to occur involves "the blurring of the borders between the logic of facts and the logic of fictions."[8] Thus, for Rancière, rather than guide a viewer toward a particular response or action, the move of presenting fact and fiction on the same perceptual schematic takes on a radical political valence by prompting a rethinking of the forms of visibility and intelligibility in which inequalities are embedded. In short, Rancière sees political art as facilitating "material rearrangements of signs and images, relations between what can be seen and what is said, between what is done and what can be done."[9]

The Toohey's joker, by contrast with "Elmo," compresses, rather than amplifies, the distinction between enunciation and the enunciated. His act of enunciation (the straight-faced uttering of the question, "What have they given me?") enters into the enunciation itself, thus providing the comic twist. Indeed, the gag depends precisely upon the absurdity created by this implausible collapse between enunciation and the enunciated. To be specific, by enacting a seamless relationship between enunciation and the enunciated at the level of form, while expressing an absurdity at the level of content, the illusion of a frictionless relationship between the two is destroyed. But the illusion of the existence of metalanguage is upheld because we unequivocally know that a stunt is being attempted, a recognition that is reinforced by the laughter that overcomes the pub worker and guests.

Neither of these particular examples succeeds in facilitating an act of aesthetic politics. Nevertheless, I will argue that realism, as an aesthetic form played out across a range of media and art, carries a potential to unsettle the conservative role of metalanguage. Central to this claim lies realism's complicity with deception. To uncover this relationship between realism and deception, we must go beyond the view of deception as a lie that is presented in the form of truth—a dissimulation in which something pretends to be something it is not. This position limits us to making comparisons between one entity and another in order to assess their similarities and differences. Instead, the deception that will interest us here is one which helps us to appreciate internal contradictions—ruses that provoke us to consider the relationship a thing has, not with another thing, but rather with itself. Such a move facilitates a concern not simply with epistemological uncertainty regarding the status of truth and falsity, but rather with ontological indeterminacy regarding the very possibility of the categories of truth and falsity. In this way, we encounter the Lacanian insight that rather than a metalanguage which guarantees meaning from outside, "the guarantee is included in, is part of what it guarantees."[10] If, as seen in these examples, both minimizing and accentuating the gap between the enunciated and the enunciation can work to prop up metalanguage's efficacy, then how might we imagine ways for it to be compromised? One approach involves demonstrating the ways in which, rather than act as language's seamless guarantor (as transparent forms of realism require), metalanguage can antagonize language. My husband's response to my first attempt at making pancakes exemplified this possibility. After taking his first bite, he remarked: "These pancakes are indistinguishable from really good pancakes!" Why could I take this as neither unequivocal praise nor, by any means, a straightforward criticism?

In this example, the act of enunciation (his uttering the statement) destabilized the truth value of the enunciated (the statement itself), creating an indeterminacy about whether my pancakes were (or could be) "indistinguishable" from "really good pancakes." Here, the enunciated content overtly claims that it is impossible to differentiate my pancakes from "really good pancakes." And yet the very fact of having made the statement invalidated its truth value: in calling them "indistinguishable" he clearly *did* distinguish them from "really good pancakes." If the statement is to be taken as "true"—that my pancakes *are* indistinguishable from really good pancakes—then we are faced with a puzzle: how can a thing be compared to itself?

The photorealist paintings by Vienna-based American artist Judith Eisler helps to set the scene for exploring, in a visual art context, the ways in which indeterminacy haunts the relationship between a thing and itself. Eisler paints flawless renditions of movie stills taken from models she derives by videotaping films, pausing on a scene, and then taking a photograph. The scenes that she reproduces contain a range of visual distortions which emerge from the processes of mechanical reproduction: refractions of light, blurred backgrounds, and even the pixelated line of interference that can appear when a videotape has been paused midframe. Eisler, in an impeccably realistic way, paints the disturbances that must go unnoticed in order for the transparent realism of mainstream cinema to be effective.

She cunningly deploys the "subjective" medium of painting (a form whose claims to realism occur only at the iconic level) in order to create perfect mimetic copies of (imperfect) images created by the mechanical, "objective," media forms (forms which offer indexical connections to profilmic reality). But she adds a twist that takes her work further into the realm of the simulacrum than her peers: she perfectly reproduces the disturbances caused precisely by intrusions of the technical apparatuses of cinema, photography, and video recorders. Eisler's paintings thus might be seen as providing a too perfect resemblance to their mediated precursors. By foregrounding the role of deception normally hidden in realist works, Eisler skillfully executes perfect verisimilitude—a key tool in the creation of the realist illusion—but now in the service of unsettling claims to realism. These paintings challenge the illusion of metalanguage by entrusting a subjective art form to not only carry out an impeccable verisimilitude but also to highlight the glitches which arise from the intrusion of mechanical apparatuses into the realist illusion.

The activist art collective Not an Alternative provides us with an example of a more overtly political aesthetic intervention along these lines.[11] They are the organization perhaps best known for creating what they call "Occupy Tape," a variation on the familiar cautionary yellow and black tape which police use to cordon off areas of danger. Not an Alternative used "Occupy Tape" to mark off areas where Occupy Wall Street protests were taking place. From a distance, Not an Alternative's "Occupy Tape" appears "real"—identical to the police tape; only up close does the word in black writing register: "occupy." The tape played a key role during the Occupy movements in New York and beyond, functioning, I claim, as what James F. Lastra, following Denis Hollier, calls a strategy of "equivocation."[12] Such an intervention operates in terms of what Lastra describes as "'a mimetic subversion' that appropriates and diverts the enemy's slogans, that claims to outstrip him on his own grounds, to combat him with his own weapons."[13]

The effectiveness of Not an Alternative's creation can be measured only in part by moments in which passersby confused the Occupy tape with the "real" thing. Its true success can be better appreciated when the inverse occurred—when passersby of a "real" police matter assume from a distance that the tape must indicate that an area is being "Occupied." Here, rather than a simple dissimulation, Not an Alternative ingeniously stages a trompe l'oeil. At first glance, the tape appears to be the familiar cautionary tape used by police to restrict access to areas. Yet, upon closer inspection, this mimetic similarity gives way to the inverse recognition that the areas being marked are ones inviting the public to take back public spaces in the name of anticorporate interests. Such a possibility puts in flux the authoritarian power of police caution tape.

The contributions of Not an Alternative and the work of Judith Eisler open up possibilities for thinking about the relationship between realism and deception as operating beyond the level of simple dissimulation. Richard Allen characterizes the deception undertaken by most photorealist paintings as a form of trompe l'oeil. This genre tends to conform to Jacques Lacan's description of trompe l'oeil as a painting that "captures our attention and delights us . . . at the moment when we realize that . . . [it is] something other than what it seemed."[14] But unlike traditional trompe l'oeil, the confusion that occurs with photorealism is not between representation and reality (whether, for example, we have encountered a painting of a window or an actual window) but rather one between one medium and another (whether we are looking at an actual photograph or a painting of a photograph). Allen refers to this particular phenomenon as prompting "a loss of medium awareness."[15] Drawing upon Fredric Jameson's insights, Brian Massumi takes this "loss of medium awareness" further by claiming that it launches photorealism into the register of the "simulacrum": in photorealism, "the painting is a copy not of reality, but of a photograph, which is already a copy of the original."[16] He emphasizes how the simulacral structure of "cop[ies] of cop[ies]" calls into question the very status of the "original" itself: the "relationship to the model has become so attenuated that it can no longer properly be said to be a model."[17]

Allen introduces a key distinction between illusions that create "epistemic" deceptions and illusions that operate only at a "sensory" level. For Allen, trompe l'oeil and "reproductive illusions" (his term for forms of mechanically or electronically created images in which a "fictional referent" is mistaken for "an actual one") create epistemic deceptions. In these cases, he tells us, viewers are led to confuse a fiction for reality. "Sensory illusions," by contrast, are created by visual representations that resemble things in the real world and lead viewers to experience sensory and affective responses to them without being deceived into thinking that they are real. Cinema, for Allen, can be characterized as a "projective illusion," which operates at the sensory level. Viewers can experience a film "as if it is a fully realized world" without forgetting that they are watching a film and not real life. In what follows, I will extend this framework beyond consideration of "sensory" and "epistemic" illusions to include deceptions that create *ontological* conundrums which call into question not only the relationship of the representation to the object but which also prompt consideration of the relationship of the object to itself. In such cases, the confusion lies no longer in our inability to "know" what is real and what is fiction, but rather lies in an indeterminacy regarding the distinction between the real and the fictional.

To develop this view further, we turn again to Allen, who locates the distinction between "projective illusion" and trompe l'oeil in the status of the object for which the representation is mistaken. Here, he claims, that while trompe l'oeil provokes a viewer to experience a visual representation as a "real object" (be it a window or a photograph), in a "projective illusion" "the reality experienced is a 'virtual one.'"[18] Jean Baudrillard makes a similar claim when he contends that trompe l'oeil functions in opposition to straightforward virtuality, which, rather than calling upon a viewer to question her reality, works to preserve her grip on reality. In particular, Baudrillard praises trompe l'oeil for its transgressive ability to "subtract" from reality; conversely, he condemns virtuality for its propagation of a given reality. Virtuality, he contends, "brings the play of illusion to an end through the perfection of reproduction, the virtual reissuing of the real. . . . On the contrary, *trompe l'oeil, by removing a dimension from real* objects, makes their presence magical and restores dreams, total unreality in its minute exactness."[19] By advocating for the subtraction of reality from the world, Baudrillard is not calling for nihilism, or (to use Rancière's terms) the complete destruction of the sensible world. Rather, Baudrillard is interested in the ways in which such interplay between presence and absence might create the potential to see reality in a new way, perhaps reveal new possible organizations of the sensible world. As he cautions, "each image must take away from the reality of the world . . . but one must not give in to the temptation of annihilation . . . the disappearance must remain active: that is the secret of art and seduction."[20] By "actively" playing with disappearance and the removal of reality, one temporarily suspends one's sense of reality's stability.

Trompe l'oeil, I suggest, is only one form of deception capable of achieving this playful undermining of reality. I will consider three other modes of deception that facilitate such a response. The first mode, which incorporates trompe l'oeil, operates through the creation of an illusion. For Baudrillard, a scene from the Peking Opera Company exemplifies the triumph of illusion over virtuality: "With the mere dual movement of two bodies in a skiff, an entire stretch of river is brought to life . . . there the illusion was total . . . precisely because any realist presence . . . had been eliminated. . . . It is always by adding to the real, by adding real to real in order to create the perfect illusion (the illusion of resemblance, the realist stereotype) that illusion is thoroughly killed. . . . Virtuality . . . by creating a realist image . . . destroys this illusion."[21] It is only through restraint, in the refusal to produce mimetic replicas, that this illusion could be sustained.

Baudrillard suggests that such restraint is rare in contemporary times, in which we tend to favor virtuality over illusion. In a modern version of the same scene, he speculates that "tons of water would flood the stage."[22] Such a literal display of reality would rob the scene of any desire in much the same way that pornography, "by adding a dimension to the image of sex, removes something from the dimension of desire and disqualifies any seductive illusion."[23] A gap or imperfection is required for the inauguration of desire and with it the play of absence and presence that engages the spectator in a potentially destabilizing game of seduction. Eisler's work may be seen as functioning within this destabilizing paradigm by creating apparent gems of virtuality through meticulous precision of detail, only to undercut the possibility of straightforward realism through the perfect rendering of realism's limitations. In this way, her work succeeds in creating the gap necessary for seductive illusion rather than a straightforward virtuality.

The second mode of deception that may undermine reality can be called "hypervirtuality." This category involves the creation of impeccable verisimilitude (without markers of realism's glitches, which characterize Eisler's work), in which a representation appears so real that it becomes uncannily disturbing. Naomi Schor describes how this phenomenon of the excessively real can function as an "extreme form of mimesis" which "'violate[s] our sense of reality'. . . [by] being so realistic.'"[24] Although Baudrillard indicts virtuality for being reality confirming, he celebrates *hyper*virtuality for its ability to challenge viewers' sense of reality.

This possibility emerges because the attempt to show everything confronts viewers with the disturbing awareness that it is impossible to "see it all." But here the impossibility of "seeing it all" appears to stem from epistemological constraints, rather than the more confronting prospect of this constraint occurring as a limit in reality itself.

The two modes of deception discussed earlier, trompe l'oeil and hypervirtuality, may create only minimal and fleeting disturbances to reality. They are too easily inscribed back into the symbolic realm. Our shock at the "too real" that emerges in hypervirtuality indicates, paradoxically, an awareness that these representations must not be real at all. If true mimetic perfection was achieved, these representations would be of minimal interest to spectators; unless their status as replicas was announced, they would come to be confused with the banal reality that they duplicated. For a "'shock' effect" to occur, one must realize that the representation, although appearing to be real, is most certainly *not* real. If we do not know, for example, that a window we pass is indeed a trompe l'oeil painting, we will likely regard it with indifference. For trompe l'oeil to be successful, there has to be something about it that strikes us as not quite right—some signal of artifice that arrests our attention. The acknowledgment of the distinction between artifice and reality, and, in particular, the ability to confidently adjudicate the division between the two, maintains the security of reality. Here we see that the recognition necessary for the illusion to take hold is the same recognition that is responsible for the destruction of the illusion. These forms invite us to take pleasure in playing with the line between reality and illusion, while leaving both categories intact. Thus, both of these forms of deception—trompe l'oeil and hypervirtuality—engage us in an epistemological game: to be fooled or entertained by their realist status, we must know that they are really not real. In Rancière's terms, for these forms to work, we must have "knowledge of our ignorance."[25]

This recognition can be used to resolve a puzzle posed by Barbara Creed regarding the appeal of virtual reality. Creed points out that "through the powers of virtual reality, the individual may enter a cyber world which is indistinguishable from the real world."[26] This possibility, she continues, raises "one of the key paradoxes of virtual reality": "If the virtual world is impossible to distinguish from the real world, why go there in the first place?"[27] Creed then attempts to account for the allure of virtual reality in terms of the freedom it offers one to "enter and leave at will, adopt a new identity, establish relations. . . . The virtual world offers flexibility, fluidity, fantasy."[28] But this explanation should be taken further. The virtual world may be indistinguishable from the real world if one considers the world only in terms of its "content." But, as Creed's explanation itself reveals, it is the "form" of engagement that distinguishes the virtual world from the real world. Once form is introduced, the paradox itself dissolves: the appeal of the virtual world is precisely that it is distinguishable from the real world—and more so, we confidently *know* that it is different. Perhaps, then, a key reason why one might "go there" is to benefit from its reality-confirming effects.

The third category of deception takes the form of what Baudrillard refers to as "simulation." Common interpretations of simulation (or simulacrum, as he sometimes calls it) locate it on the side of virtuality—as a perfected form of virtual reality. For Baudrillard, by contrast, simulation is a form of deception that belongs on the side of illusion not virtuality. I, thus, use the notion of "true simulation" to refer to a simulation based on illusion, which creates indeterminacy regarding its status as reality.

Baudrillard, we have seen, favors illusion over virtuality, because the former carries the transgressive potential of unsettling the principles of reality, whereas the latter ultimately works to secure the realist illusion. The contention that simulations operate as a form of illusion rather than virtuality, however, meets with apparent difficulty because as Baudrillard warns, a "true simulation" risks being confused with reality. This caution seems to imply that simulation belongs on the side of the virtual, because it is in the realm of virtuality that the seamless replication of reality is sought. However, my position emphasizes that the confusion with reality that a true simulation causes cannot be settled by accruing knowledge regarding its epistemological status. The confusion created by a true simulation occurs not at the level of knowledge, but rather at the level of being. In this sense, a true simulation is ontologically indeterminate rather than merely epistemologically uncertain.

Unlike forms of dissimulation, in which the false is presented as true, a "true simulation," for Baudrillard, renders notions of true and false inoperative and undecidable. He explains, for example, that one can "dissimulate" being ill "by going to bed" and surrounding oneself with crumpled-up tissues and cups of tea. In such a scenario, one can be discovered to have been pretending. But, if one wishes to "truly" simulate illness, then one must "produce 'true' symptoms" of the illness, which raises doubt about whether we can say that the person is indeed ill or not.[29] A "true simulation" of illness makes the health status of the person simulating an illness not merely uncertain, but truly indeterminate. In short, against the standard interpretation of simulation as a virtuality that enhances reality, a true simulation functions as a radical illusion that subtracts from reality in the sense of placing an element of reality outside the domain of truths or falsehoods, and thus outside the domain of knowledge. What happens when knowledge is not possible, not because of a failure at the level of epistemology, but because of an ontological impasse, created in a true simulation? This question, as well as the more general question of the possible relationships of deception to the impression of realism and their attendant political stakes, lies at the heart of this book.

OVERVIEW

This book circulates the key question of how political transformation might be facilitated by disruptive encounters from within the realm of the aesthetic—in particular, within the much maligned aesthetic category of realism. More specifically, through a study of recent trends within cinema, television, and contemporary art, I propose to investigate the question of how the realist aesthetic form might be used to create disturbances within the existing symbolic order. This project challenges the enduring position that the realist form operates on the side of stability and thus is complicit with ideological conservatism. As Colin MacCabe, a frequent exporter of this view that realism is a "'predominantly conservative form'" argues, it "'fixes the subject in a point of view from which everything becomes obvious.'"[30]

According to this traditional position, realism's political role has been limited to serving consciousness-raising politics through its ability to guide the spectator toward previously unseen truths by lifting the veil of ideological deception. This position would see the political possibilities in "Elmo's" performance as dependent upon revealing what lies behind its fiction. In what follows, I reject this approach, which is predicated on the assumption that by seeing through the ideological fictions that conceal the true workings of an institution, we undermine them. Following Slavoj Žižek, I contend that such revelations strengthen rather than weaken the force of ideological illusion. Enabling spectators to "see through" a fiction creates a scene ripe for the acceptance of greater deception because viewers feel they are now securely "in the know." Ideology is most effective when it creates the impression that we know better and therefore are immune to its influence. Of additional concern, this traditional premise perpetuates the illusion that ideology operates in the deep recesses of content, rather than on the surface, through a representation's form. Rather than seek to unearth the truth behind the fiction, this book argues that we would do well to turn our attention to the truth *of* the fiction.

In particular, my main contention will be that realism's political potential emerges not from revealing deceptions but rather from "staging" deceptions—particularly deceptions that imperil the very categories of true and false. In arguing for this view, I contest two prevailing (yet diametrically opposed) currents within film theory that take up the relationship between realism and deception: (1) indictments of filmic realism for deceptively creating illusions that are mistaken for reality; and (2) celebrations of cinematic realism for its unique ability to expose the deception inherent in the construction of hegemonic narratives. By contrast with position (1), I argue that deception functions not as an obstacle to truth, but rather as a necessary lure for snaring the truth. And although I share with position (2) the belief that filmic realism can contribute to a political aesthetics, I locate this potential not in film's ability to simply reveal what has been concealed, but rather in its more radical capacity to disrupt the given perceptual framework through which such suppressions occur.

The key thinkers whose insights I build upon in developing this argument are Jacques Lacan and Jacques Rancière. In particular, I draw upon the Lacanian provocation that truth can only emerge through deception. In opposition to Frankfurt School–inspired film theorists who assail the cinematic tendency to present a false reality as if it were true, Lacan helps us to see that truth itself is the product of a lie. In this formulation, it is only by giving up the possibility of adjudicating truth from a point existing outside of fiction that one can properly arrive at truth.

Rancière has emerged as a central figure in the development of an aesthetics politics. He rejects a traditional politics of the image based on consciousness raising in which images are thought to "make viewers aware of the structures of domination and inspire them to mobilize their energies."[31] Hence, for Rancière, the political potential of the realist form lies not in its ability "to counter-pose reality to its appearances," but rather "to construct different realities, different forms of common sense."[32] More specifically, for Rancière, an aesthetics politics is achieved by creating a "dissensus"— the unsettling of naturalized systems of perception that, by masking the exclusions upon which the impression of such a totality depends, perpetuate the illusion of total inclusivity. Thus, the political project put forth by Rancière does not merely seek to give voice and representational privilege to those who have been marginalized within a given system but instead requires challenging the very configurations of the sensible through which such exclusions occur.

My project both builds upon and extends these Lacanian and Rancièrian insights in seeking to explore recent filmic, televisual, and artistic works (performance/installation/sculpture) as well as cultural practices (breastfeeding) that, I will argue, present us with ripe material for imagining the potentially transformative possibilities of "disorder." These explorations, I will argue, help to bring to light the following significant confluence between the work of Lacan and Rancière: both thinkers highlight the ways in which the very system of order ("the symbolic," for Lacan and the "sensible" for Rancière) gives rise to disorder ("the Real" for Lacan, and "dissensus" for Rancière). For Lacan, for example, the disruptive category of "the Real" emerges through the failure of the symbolic system to fully and without remainder represent all of "reality." One way to define the Real is as the remainder of this project of representation. Thus, by contrast with frequent characterizations of the Real as a terrifying Thing that *causes* the symbolic system to stumble, Lacan emphasizes that the Real is the *effect* of the constitutive failure of the symbolic to flawlessly render reality. Rancière, similarly, emphasizes that one should not look to external phenomenon for disturbances to the sensible, but rather to the internal logic of the representative regime itself. For Rancière, disorder emerges as an artifact of the constraints that govern the representational system. These fundamental insights provide the theoretical underpinning of the argument of this book: namely, that efforts to produce realist representations give rise to the destabilizing Real.

In arguing this, I draw upon a range of art and media examples with the aim of teasing out particular relationships between realism and deception that maximize this potential for realism to disrupt ideological formations. In Chapter 1, I analyze the sculptural figures created by Australian artist Ron Mueck, which appear, at the level of corporeal content, as unimpeachable examples of the perfected mimetic form, yet at the level of scale, as eerily flawed. I will argue that Mueck's use of scale to disrupt the illusion of perfected reality illuminates ways in which realist forms of art carry the political potential to open up opportunities for new ways of seeing, understanding, and being in the world.

Chapter 2 considers two recent films, *Catfish* (Ariel Schulman and Henry Joust) and *This Is Not a Film* (Jafar Panahi), with a view to arguing how the most prized indicators of filmic realism can function as signs of lapses in the realist edifice. I argue that such signs function as pointers to the elusive truth characteristic of what I call "Real-ism"—that is, hints of the Real that emerges precisely when the symbolic framework governing reality becomes imperiled.

Chapter 3 takes up the controversy surrounding Yale University senior Aliza Shvarts, who made international headlines when reports circulated that her senior-year art project documented a year in which she frequently tried to impregnate herself while taking herbs to induce a miscarriage. At the heart of the uproar lies a fundamental uncertainty as to the nature of the documented event. In particular, claims that the piece was a "hoax" imply that she performed a mere dissimulation rather than, as Shvartz herself suggests, a true simulation. This case also serves as an opportunity to assess the political implications of artistic forms in which tensions between claims of realism and deception emerge, and it helps us to attend to difficulties encountered in the deployment of both dissimulation and simulation as strategies for upsetting the social order.

Chapter 4 explores "Bitte liebt Österreich" ("Please Love Austria"), the controversial public art installation created by the late German conceptual artist and provocateur Christoph Schlingensief. Schlingensief staged a variation on the reality TV show, *Big Brother*, in which asylum seekers were housed in a structure in a public square in Vienna, Austria. Passersby were invited to cast their vote each night for which detainee should be evicted the following day. By staging his intervention as a "game" that borrowed from the familiar "reality TV" genre, Schlingensief invites us to consider the question of whether using a fictional, game-like, mode of representation to describe a politically reactionary event may help to subvert it. He thus offers an important twist to the logic which undergirds the position that realistic depictions of revolutionary events can themselves be politically potent.

Chapter 5 continues with the theme of reality television, but here in terms of a comparison between a series of made-for-TV movies based around "true events" and "real people," and the faux reality TV show *The Joe Schmo Show*. The premise of this show rests upon a cast of actors convincing an earnest participant that he is involved in a *Big Brother*–style reality TV show. I argue that, unlike the first set of docu-dramas which enable viewers to "see through" the fictionalized scene, *Joe Schmo* functions in an unexpectedly disruptive way. Through setting up a seemingly irresistible scene for "seeing through" the ruse and then exploiting its attendant traps, the show accomplishes the subversive task of undermining the power of the ideological call of mastery associated with the realist form.

In Chapter 6, I compare two realist representations of the human body: *Körperweltern (BodyWorlds)*, Gunther Von Hagens's unprecedented public display of chemically preserved human corpses, and *Cloaca*, Belgian artist Wim Delvoye's electromechanical replication of the functions of the human digestive system from ingestion to excretion. A comparison between these two displays points to the unexpected way in which the droll defecating machine creates more of a disturbance to the categories of true and false and human and inhuman than does the display that stages a confrontation between living spectators and dead human bodies.

Chapter 7 extends explorations of representations of the human body through an examination of two prominent discursive sites concerning contemporary practices of breastfeeding, the US government's 2004 National Breastfeeding Awareness Campaign and La Leche League International. Here, rather than an overt engagement with reality and deception, we encounter the way in which the Real haunts accounts of the body that aim to firmly ground themselves within the Symbolic realm (the national campaign) and the Imaginary realm (La Leche).

I conclude the book with a return to film, namely Lars von Trier's *Melancholia*, in which we are presented with the story of a profoundly depressed woman on the brink of the apocalypse. This film, I argue, demonstrates the ethical priority of embracing the constitutive power of illusion.

In conducting this investigation, I bridge methodological approaches of different disciplines. In particular, I draw upon a range of scholarship from within art history, literary studies, political theory, psychoanalysis, and film studies. My overarching methodology, however, stems from a commitment to the imbrication of the empirical and the theoretical. I perform close readings of cultural artifacts that combine visual/filmic analysis with accounts of their reception. But rather than simply apply theoretical frameworks to the examples, I engage also in the reverse move of using the "cases" to illuminate the theory. The empirical, in this sense, guarantees that theory itself be subject to the same level of scrutiny under which it places its objects.

CHAPTER 1

The Realistically Deceptive, or the Deceptively Real? Ron Mueck and the Internal Illusion

Realism, as an aesthetic form, has long been indicted for its complicity with ideological conservatism. This chapter aims to make a case for a reconsideration of realism as a critical tool in the formation of contemporary aesthetic politics. In developing this claim, I draw upon Jacques Rancière's insights regarding the potential for aesthetic formations to take on a political dimension by "introducing into [our sense of community] new subjects and objects, ... render[ing] visible what had not been, and ... mak[ing] heard as speakers those who had been perceived as mere noisy animals."[1] Such shifts in our capacity to envision new realities can change "the landscape of the possible" by rupturing anticipated correlations between images and their meanings and images and their effects.[2]

An aesthetic politics, in Rancière's sense, requires a shift from the "representative regime" of art to what he calls the "aesthetic regime." For Rancière, this transition must no longer be understood as a simple break with mimetic realism in favor of nonfigurative art. As he puts it, "the break with [the representational regime] does not consist in painting white squares rather than ... warriors."[3] Rather than discarding figurative art, this break requires giving up the idea that a representational form carries what he calls an "expressive complement," such as that between "a lion and courage."[4] More specifically, the break from the representative to the aesthetic regime involves for Rancière the recognition that an image can no longer be simply understood as a "codified expression of a thought or feeling."[5] Such codified meanings, he argues, reproduce the status quo by limiting the ability of things to exist in ways that have not yet been thought and thus suppress the potential to bring to life possible new ways of being. This chapter follows Rancière in refusing to claim that realist forms of art are inconsistent with a political aesthetics. My main contention will be that realism's potential political power lies not in its ability to guide the spectator toward previously unseen truths or to see through deception. Rather, its potential emerges by staging deceptions that imperil any recourse to the metalanguage that sustains the very categories of true and false, thereby undermining the possibility of belief and the system of authority that it secures. To put this more generally in Rancièrian terms, realism's charge in the project of aesthetic politics is to conspire with deception in order to dispute the established regime of representation and generate what he calls a new "distribution of the sensible," through which new organizations of perception may emerge.[6]

In the course of this chapter, I consider a series of art and media examples that, in increasingly complex ways, address the political question of how to create a new distribution of the sensible by undermining the structure of belief and the system of authority (the big Other, in Lacanian parlance) that sustain the given arrangement.[7] I illustrate this politics through the sculptural figures created by Ron Mueck, which, I argue, innovatively harness the potentially transformative moment when the established perceptual framework begins to fray. In particular, Mueck's use of scale to disrupt the illusion of reality illuminates ways in which realist forms of art carry the political potential to open up opportunities for new ways of seeing, understanding, and being in the world. His sculptures, we will see, do this by inaugurating a new twist on conventional trompe l'oeil by reproducing, at the level of context, the deception that traditionally occurs only at the level of form.

BELIEF, DOUBT, AND THE BIG OTHER

At first sight, the sculptural figures produced by Australian artist Ron Mueck appear as unimpeachable examples of the perfected mimetic form. At the level of detail, his pieces are ultrarealist in their corporeal renderings, as seen, for example, in the stray hairs that cling to the blotchy face of the woman who is just moments past giving birth in *Mother and Child*. Yet at the level of scale, these figures are eerily flawed. Perhaps most disturbing in this regard is *Dead Dad*, Mueck's impeccable translation of every detail of his dead father's body, from the wrinkles on the bottom of his feet to the coarse hairs barely protruding from his nose, into a figure only three-quarters of his actual size.

In the catalog to the 2003 exhibition of Mueck's sculptures at the London National Gallery, Susana Greeves credits Mueck with deceiving viewers or at least in creating a delayed recognition regarding the distorted scale he employs: "Mueck's work seems so scrupulously faithful to reality in the detail that one does not immediately notice the larger liberties he takes with . . . principles of proportion and anatomy."[8] In an analysis of the work of Duane Hanson, a sculptor to whom Mueck is often compared, Naomi Schor makes a similar claim: "The 'finer details' [in Hanson's case of clothing, accessories, and bearing] . . . catch and hold the spectator's gaze. . . . [T]he fascination they exert on the spectator prevents him from focusing on his doubt" regarding their reality.[9] Through these accounts it would seem that Mueck and Hanson practice a specific form of realist art, one in which the lure of the real delays or distracts us from the recognition of artifice, which, in the case of Mueck, is not simply present through the pieces' status as inanimate objects but is also reinforced through inhuman distortions at the level of scale. In the standard logic of dissimulation, a fabrication is intended to be accepted as real. According to these commentators, in a slight twist on this usual formula, both Mueck and Hanson prompt viewers to recognize that their fabrications are indeed fabrications but, as in trompe l'oeil, do so only after a brief delay, during which spectators entertain the possibility of the reality of the works, or at least an appreciation of their hyperrealistic status.

Greeves's and Schor's argument implies that if we could put on permanent hold our doubt about the reality of the works, we would more fully believe in their reality—that full belief presupposes freedom from doubt. By contrast, following Slavoj Žižek, I argue that against expectation, doubt functions not as an impediment to belief but rather as belief's necessary condition of possibility.[10] Doubt, in the Žižekian formulation, secures rather than undermines belief. This means that in order to sabotage belief, one must create certainty not about a reality that contradicts what one believes but instead certainty that *confirms* the very thing that one believes. Certainty sabotages belief by erasing the doubt that belief requires.

A Lacanian framework helps us to appreciate the necessary connection between belief and doubt and how belief, in turn, holds together the social-symbolic network, which secures the status of the big Other. As Žižek puts it, "the status of the Lacanian big Other *qua* symbolic institution is that of belief (trust), not that of knowledge."[11] However, belief, in this context, enjoys a peculiar status. It never takes the form of a direct relationship but rather only occurs at a distance. When we believe, we do not think that *we* believe—rather, we take up the position of doubt. What we believe when we believe is not our own belief, but rather that there is another—the "subject supposed to believe"—who *really* believes, thereby freeing us to doubt. Thus, Žižek describes belief as "always minimally 'reflective,' a 'belief in the belief of the other. . . . In order for the belief to function, there *has to be* some ultimate guarantor of it, yet this guarantor is always deferred, displaced, never present *in persona*."[12] Žižek illustrates the way this externalization of belief operates through the example of Niels Bohr hanging a good-luck horseshoe outside of his house. When guests expressed surprise that Bohr believed in such superstition, he is said to have replied that of course he did not believe it, but he was told that it was supposed to work even "if one does not believe in it."[13]

This phenomenon is well illustrated by the 2007 film *Lars and the Real Girl* (dir. Craig Gillespie), which provides a moving example of the key role that belief plays in stitching together social-symbolic reality. Lars (Ryan Gosling), a sweet but shy and lonely man, orders a life-sized blow-up doll that he pretends is his real girlfriend, whom he calls Bianca. The degree to which he believes in her reality is left somewhat ambiguous, but what is significant is that *others* around him believe that he believes. Although the deception is unsuccessful in the sense that others remain unconvinced that Bianca is real, it is nonetheless energetically maintained by Lars's family and friends who, under the advice of his psychologist, go to great lengths to prop up the illusion that Bianca is real. By providing them with the necessary alibi, the psychologist frees them to believe. They act as if Bianca is real, since her presence does wonders in transforming Lars into a confident social being. The community carries out Lars's belief so thoroughly and successfully that when Bianca is no longer a necessary prop for Lars's transformation, he is unable to let go of the ruse. The only way out for Lars is to arrange for Bianca's death. He must preserve his belief in Bianca in order to safeguard the big Other *qua* social-symbolic reality of the community to which he belongs, a reality that is built around belief, specifically a belief in his belief.

Here, however, a point of tension in Žižek's work surfaces—one that both highlights the resilience of the big Other and gestures toward a tactic for undermining its socially conservative function. Žižek contends that the big Other *qua* the "subject supposed to believe" functions as the "fundamental, constitutive feature of the symbolic order" and that "all concrete versions of this 'subject supposed to believe' . . . are stand-ins for the big Other."[14] Let us consider this assertion in relation to a point he makes in his *In Defense of Lost Causes*. In addressing Lacan's radical claim that "there is no big Other," Žižek contends that although such a view "has now become commonplace it may very well be that the opposite is true, that 'the big Other' is more present than ever."[15] Perhaps it is not the big Other that is missing, he suggests, but rather "a small other which would embody, stand in for, the big Other."[16] He explains that in postmodern times, "every small other is ... perceived as fallible, imperfect, 'merely human', ridiculous ... [and] inadequate to give body to a big Other." But, he argues, such criticism of the figures who stand in for the big Other not only fails to undermine the big Other but also unwittingly "preserve[s] the purity of the big Other unblemished by its failings." From this observation, Žižek concludes that "the task of radical politics is, therefore, not to denounce the inadequacy of every small other to stand in for the big Other (such a 'critique' only reinforces the big Other's hold over us) but to undermine the very big Other and in this way to untie the social bond the big Other sustains."

I argue for such a radical politics along Rancièrian lines that, rather than aiming for the total dissolution of the social bond, seeks to exploit the political potential offered by the instability of the big Other. This instability, in turn, makes possible a breaking apart of the representative regime sustaining the established social hierarchy. Drawing from Rancière, the goal is not total anomie, however, but instead is a shift within the established perceptual framework, which allows what has been invisible to come to light. What are some possible tactics for undertaking this political task?

Perhaps Lacan's insights regarding the relationship between the penis and the phallus might provide a model for such a tactic. For Lacan, the authority of the phallus is compromised not by denouncing the penis as an *inadequate* embodiment of the phallus but instead by exposing that the ordinary penis, in all its inadequacy, is precisely the *appropriate* representative for the phallus. To function as a symbol of power, the phallus requires the invisibility of the penis. As Lacan puts it, the phallus "can play its role only when veiled."[17] In short, the penis's effective invisibility within the dominant cultural image repertoire plays a key role in securing phallic power. Susan Bordo emphasizes this Lacanian point by suggesting that the exposure of real penises can "haunt phallic authority, threaten its undoing."[18]

Might a similar tactic be applied here in the exposure of ordinary small others who personify the big Other? By recognizing that pathetic small others, like Lars for example, *do* embody the big Other, can we contribute to dismantling the mystique that secures the big Other's power and thus work toward the radical political project that Žižek envisions? The recognition that these seemingly unworthy creatures function successfully as guardians of the symbolic pact would seem to call the bluff of the big Other's authority and undermine its power in much the same way that the exposure of the penis compromises phallic authority. Despite the temptation of this analogy, this mode of undermining the power of the phallus fails as a tactic for undercutting the binding force of the big Other, but this failure points us in a more promising direction.

Unlike the ability of the exposed penis to diminish the power of the phallus, the exposure of the inadequacies of the small others who embody the big Other does not work to loosen the social bond that the big Other sustains. To extend Žižek's insight, not only does the denunciation of flawed small others as unworthy incarnates of the big Other lend support to the big Other's authority, so too (paradoxically) does the acknowledgment that these flawed small others successfully embody the big Other. Why? To draw upon another Žižekian insight, ideology works by creating the impression that we are outside of it, superior to it. By fostering a feeling that we know better and can see through its conceits, ideology *implicates*, rather than extricates, subjects from its grip. It follows that the charming naïveté of a character such as Lars provides us with an ideal figure upon which we can displace our beliefs, because our very feeling of distance and superiority maintains our sense that we don't really believe. Rather than being undermined, the big Other is *upheld* through its embodiment by flawed small others. Consideration of this point will suggest a different tactic for compromising the power of the big Other by undermining the system of authority that sustains belief.

When, on rare occasions, an admired authority figure or a person with power (someone who might seem to be a more appropriate substitute for the big Other) becomes a subject who really believes in what he or she does—becomes "the subject supposed to believe"—the binding power of the big Other finds itself compromised. More generally, if we think that an other to whom we can relate (or with whom we aspire to compare ourselves) *really* believes—that is, believes beyond a shadow of a doubt what we are supposed to believe (but really doubt)—we often encounter discomforting anxiety. The necessary distance and doubt for maintaining our belief have then become compromised. This suggests that a viable tactic for realizing Žižek's vision for a radical political intervention based on the dissolution of the big Other is to emphasize the rare examples where the big Other is embodied not by an inadequate small other but instead by a small other who is beyond reproach (e.g., a truly infallible pope or in some cases, perhaps, political leaders in their honeymoon phase). Here, it might seem, removing the possibility of doubt functions as a disruption of the Other.

But this second tactic flirts with a temptation against which Žižek cautions: one must resist the trap of attempting to undermine belief by transforming it into knowledge through the replacement of doubt with certainty. Such replacement of belief by certainty, he argues, fuels the reactionary modes of both fundamentalism and cynicism and thus falls short of undermining the socially binding structure of belief upon which the big Other's authority depends. This tactic shares the problem illustrated by Žižek's example of scientifically validating the Shroud of Turin: the reduction of belief to mere knowledge through objective confirmation diminishes rather than enhances its authority. Paradoxically, however, as we saw earlier when we considered the exposure of the penis as a means of undermining phallic authority, the opposite path of attempting to undermine belief by objectively *invalidating* what one believes (even when one does not believe that one believes it) is also inadequate. Both of these tactics fail because they share the same logic: they operate by deploying knowledge (either positively or negatively) as the mechanism for eroding belief.

A third and more promising tactic for destabilizing the authority binding together the established social order entails undermining belief, not through the epistemological tactics of producing or challenging certainty, but instead through the creation of an *ontological* enigma. Jean Baudrillard's example of a simulated illness, discussed in the introduction, highlights the way such ontological challenges erode the grounding principles of reality in ways that belief cannot rescue. For Baudrillard, a "true simulation" of an illness requires that one must "produce 'true' symptoms" of the illness.[19] But, he points out, such simulation makes indeterminate whether the person is indeed ill or not and thus, it seems, eliminates the possibility of knowledge. This, in turn, I suggest, undermines the possibility of belief, because the (unfulfilled) prospect of knowledge is necessary to sustaining belief. Once knowledge is no longer possible, belief is compromised. In other words, for belief to take hold there must be the always deferred possibility of certainty and, thus, knowledge. In Žižek's terms, belief "can only thrive in the shadowy domain between outright falsity and positive truth."[20] Because it implies the failure of exactly this distinction between truth and falsity, Baudrillard's notion of "true simulation" provides us with a key model for realizing this sort of ontological enigma that destabilizes authority.

But, as I indicated in the Introduction, the project of creating a successful "true" simulation—one that realizes its reality-shattering potential—faces a key difficulty: if it is successful, it will be mistaken for reality. Consider, for example, Baudrillard's question of what the police would make of a "simulated" holdup. Even with harmless weapons and a hostage who is "in the know," the simulator will nonetheless find herself "mixed up" with reality. As Baudrillard suggests, the "victim" will really give over the money, someone will have a heart attack, a police officer will fire a gun, and so on. The pragmatic difficulties of staging a successful simulation are further complicated by the efforts of those in power to deny that a simulation has occurred. As Baudrillard contends, "the repressive apparatus would ... react MORE violently to a simulated hold up than [to] a real one."[21] A "real hold up," he argues, "only upsets the order of things ... whereas a simulated hold up interferes with the very principle of reality." In other words, for Baudrillard, a simulated crime poses a much greater disturbance to law and order than a real crime. A real crime emerges as an aberration that reinforces existing law and order, whereas a simulated crime "suggests ... that law and order themselves might really be nothing more than a simulation." As a result, when faced with a true simulation, holders of power work to "reinject realness and referentiality everywhere, in order to convince us of the reality of the social."

It therefore seems that if this third tactic for threatening belief and the system of authority that sustains it is to work, we must consider avenues for creating ontological indeterminacy other than a Baudrillardian simulation. In the next section I consider a fourth possibility: the creation of an awareness of what Lacan calls the impossibility of a metalanguage. It is this approach that ultimately points us in the direction of a truly transformative tactic—one that allows the recuperation of realism as a destabilizing political aesthetic form and enables us to return with fresh understanding to the disruptive potential of Mueck's sculptures as an avatar of this new political realism.

DESTABILIZING METALANGUAGE

A stand-up routine from the New Zealand music-comedy duo Flight of the Conchords provides an opportunity to explore the possibility of undermining the role of metalanguage as a mechanism for creating indeterminacy regarding reality. In the context of a comic sketch about the impact of social problems on children, Jermaine reminds his counterpart, Brett, that his children are unlikely to be affected by social problems because Brett's children are only imaginary. Here we encounter a significant twist on the example of Lars: whereas Lars pretends to have a *real* girlfriend, Brett pretends to have *imaginary* children. This contamination of reality by the imaginary prevents us from calling upon a firm distinction between truth and fiction. Specifically, when Jermaine presses Brett on how his pretend family would be subjected to social problems, Brett maintains that the imaginary family would actually be doubly susceptible to suffering the effects of social problems, since they would have to endure both the pretend problems ("rogue unicorns," for instance) and the real problems (people not believing in their existence) that imaginary children would face. In this case, neither Jermaine nor the audience believes that Brett really believes in his pretend family. Instead, the comic banter helps to uproot the clear distinction between representation and reality: the real and the pretend intermingle on the same plane. In particular, Brett refuses to oppose reality and fantasy, and in so doing he helps to demonstrate the important Lacanian point that reality and fantasy actually exist on the same side, working in tandem to cover over the Real, to disguise the cracks in the symbolic order. For Lacan, fantasy provides the implicit coordinates that govern one's reality. Thus, rather than operate as an escape from reality, fantasy functions as reality's most vital prop. Together, reality and fantasy conspire to shield us from encountering the Real of our desire (the core of our being that threatens to shatter our symbolic existence).

It is time now to begin bringing these theoretical points together in rethinking the possibility of a political aesthetic realism. Both Brett's schtik and Lars's apparent delusion play, in different ways, with the distinction between reality and fantasy in a manner that destabilizes the possibility of coping with harsh reality by opposing it to fantasy. On the one hand, Lars's example emphasizes ways in which fantasy incorporates itself into the regime of reality. In the film, Lars's friends and family go to such lengths to accept Bianca into their real world that they set a place for her at dinner parties and find her a job—conveniently as a shop-window model for a local clothing store. But on the other hand we see too that reality must intrude into Lars's world of fantasy: for example, Lars must provide a "reasonable" explanation for why he carries Bianca around, so he constructs a narrative in which he explains that she is paralyzed.

Brett takes even further such injection of reality into the world of fantasy by subjecting fantasy to the grim reality of social problems. But he also demonstrates the ways in which reality is made to deal with fantasy. Reality can accept fantasy as its counterpart without friction only when it is safely marked as such. Thus, a pretend real girlfriend (like Bianca) is easier to accommodate in some ways (because she is comfortably framed within our expectations of a dissimulation) than a pretend "pretend" family (which challenges our expectations of both fantasy and reality). Lars's case thus reinforces both the power of reality to colonize fantasy and the role that fantasy plays in propping up reality. Brett's routine, by contrast, makes the more unsettling inverse move of pointing to the fictional status of reality itself.

One reason for this difference lies in the differing status that "belief" holds in each example. Lars embodies Lacan's proverbial "subject supposed to believe," in the sense that Lars's supposed belief in Bianca functions not only to prop up his own reality but also to stitch together reality for the larger community. In Brett and Jermaine's banter, by contrast, the subject who is supposed to believe is absent. The humor arises from going beyond the mere suspension of the role of the subject who is supposed to believe to making the suspension of belief internal to the narrative. This move works to erase the security that metalanguage confers on standard cases of dissimulation. That is, by eroding the external metalinguistic position from which we can adjudicate reality, any guarantee of symbolic efficacy is lost. When the illusion of a reliable metalanguage is shattered in this way, we are faced with the destabilizing awareness that our most binding rituals of belief have no objective or external support. In short, through the blurring of fantasy and reality, we encounter a potential disruption to the reality principle.

Finally, a scene from the BBC comedy *Love Soup* provides an occasion to explore a representation that goes further than the Flight of the Conchords example in bringing us closer to an encounter with the inability of metalanguage to confirm our reality. The scene presents us with a man and a woman undressing in anticipation of making love for the first time. As the man takes off his clothes, we see his genital region overlaid with the familiar blurry square matrix—the conventional disguise for censored images. The audience's curiosity to see what is behind the cover is intensified by the diegetic response of his companion. The woman's intense horror at what she sees seems to exceed any reasonable explanation of what might be the "reality" behind the mask. The audience is thus beautifully set up for the unexpected twist: the woman, we find out, sees exactly the same blurry matrix that we, the audience, see. When she demands an explanation, her companion anxiously explains that in his deeply religious cultish family, all boys at the age of fourteen, to preserve their modesty, get their genitals covered by a censorship matrix.[22] More shocking than any possible discovery of what is behind the blurry matrix is the fact that there is actually *nothing* behind the blurry matrix. The censorship matrix no longer functions as a representational element that stands in for something else. Instead, it operates, openly, as an example of a *Vorstellungsrepräsentanz*—an element that "takes the place of representation."[23]

As Lacan puts it, "when I am presented with a representation, I assure myself that I know quite a lot about it, I assure myself as a consciousness that knows that it is only representation, and that there is, beyond, the thing, the thing itself."[24] The exposure of the operation of the *Vorstellungsrepräsentanz* strips away these comforts by collapsing the space between the representation and the represented. In Rancière's terms, we may say that the *Vorstellungsrepräsentanz*, when "seen through," poses a significant challenge to the representative regime and contributes to a shift to the aesthetic regime by confronting spectators with the "absence of a stable relationship between exhibition and signification."[25]

But the scene from *Love Soup* goes beyond illustrating the use of deception to activate a shift from the representative to the aesthetic regime. It also succeeds in undermining our faith in metalanguage to secure a position from which we can observe a distance between sign and referent. Here we find ourselves perfectly primed to experience a disturbance similar to that of Zeuxis, in Lacan's retelling, when he asks Parrhasios to reveal what he has painted underneath the veil, only to be told that the painting he had made was the veil itself. The blurry censorship matrix deceives in a most cunning fashion: it tricks us by actually being exactly what it is (a blurry censorship matrix), when we are expecting that it will be something else (a signifier for another signifier).

TROMPE L'OEIL: FORMAL AND CONTEXTUAL

Love Soup devises a rare moment in which we find ourselves deceived by the truth. Unlike standard forms of representation that, by their very nature, involve an act of substitution (and hence an inherent duplicity), the image of the censorship matrix operates transparently. In Žižek's terms, we could say that the image lies by telling the truth. When we expect to encounter a deception but find ourselves facing the truth, we feel as if we have been tricked. For Žižek, this phenomenon of telling the truth in the guise of a lie carries disruptive potential by confronting us with the truth of the symbolic lie—namely, the discomforting recognition that there is nothing (no hidden truth) behind the fiction.

By contrast with the approach of telling the truth in the guise of a lie, Ron Mueck's work, as discussed earlier, appears real, even though we know it is artifice. For example, critic Heiner Bastian comments that when viewing Mueck's *Dead Dad*, "the small body lying on the floor seems, on the one hand, to be an entirely uninvented 'natural' image, [and] on the other, it belongs to the 'iconography' of earthly mortality which exceeds the psychological and material aspects of the dead body."[26] Perhaps, then, we could say that Mueck's pieces lie in the guise of the truth—that they appear to be impeccable specimens of corporeal reality but turn out, after an initial hesitation, to be aesthetic inventions. As Greeves describes, "Though infinitely painstaking and laborious, his absolute technical mastery is such that the technique disappears altogether, leaving us with the fact of the body itself."[27]

Such an assessment, however, too quickly glides over a crucial and yet unremarked dimension of Mueck's work: namely, the fact that his distortions in scale are redundant as markers of artifice. In addition to their distortions of scale, the overt institutionalization of his sculptures in galleries and museums firmly secures their status as artistic objects. This has a significant consequence for their political status.

At first sight, Mueck appears to play Zeuxis to *Love Soup*'s Parrahoasis. Mueck's sculptures appear as straightforward dissimulations—fictions masquerading as truth. By radically destabilizing the metalanguage that secures distinctions between fiction and the truth, Mueck's work has the potential to go beyond not only Zeuxis's mere dissimulation but also beyond Parrahoasis's traditional form of trompe l'oeil.

As the phenomenon of the ready-made shows us, even when real objects from everyday life are placed in museums without any creative manipulation, they become transformed into artistic representations. Art theorist Arthur Danto makes this point by suggesting that when actual objects are transported from "real life" into a museum setting, the object is transformed solely "by a theory of art."[28] As Danto puts it, "What in the end makes the difference between a Brillo box and a work of art consisting of a Brillo box is a certain theory of art. It is the theory that takes it up into the world of art, and keeps it from collapsing into the real object which it is."[29] For Danto, it appears that the intervention at the level of metalanguage is required for making these objects intelligible within an aesthetic space. Naomi Schor arrives at a similar position regarding the artistic future of the realist sculptural form. Schor speculates that "taken to its logical conclusion (and beyond), realism in sculpture can only self-deconstruct, give rise to a sort of metasculpture that comments on its own means of deception."[30]

Before considering the ways in which Mueck's work functions in relation to these comments, I turn very briefly to the work of the American sculptor Mark Jenkins. In a similar vein to Mueck's works, Jenkins's figures present extremely realistic renderings of the human form. But in virtue of the placement of his sculptures in the "real world" rather than in the museum, his work constitutes a significant departure from Mueck's. Although Jenkins's figures lack the "anatomical verisimilitude" that characterizes Mueck's sculptures, an unexpected, unframed encounter with a Jenkins sculpture is deeply jarring.[31] The distinctive realist elements in Jenkins's sculptures lie in their bodily comportment; they appear faultlessly human through the nuanced construction of posture and bearing. Viewers experience an initial shock in encountering, around the corner of a building, what at first sight appears to be a fellow human being bent at the waist with its backside protruding into the pedestrian's path as if vomiting or, in the case of a piece that resulted in several panicked 911 calls, a person lying motionless atop a tall commercial billboard on the side of the road. Another shock soon follows: on second look (as with conventional trompe l'oeil) Jenkins's figures contradict the principles of reality. What may have struck viewers as unquestionably real in the immediate encounter is revealed, in an eye blink's time, to be incompatible with reality, through such monumental flaws as a missing head or the defiance of gravity.

At first sight, it would seem that Jenkins's work has much in common with Mueck's regarding his use of imperfection to interrupt a potentially convincing realist illusion. Indeed, through its location outside of the regulatory environment of the museum, Jenkins's work may seem to surpass Mueck's in terms of its promise for contributing to an aesthetic politics of the sort envisioned by Rancière. To be specific, it would appear as if by existing in the context of public space rather than the museum, Jenkins's sculptures escape the reliance on metalanguage, which for Danto and Schor threatens to condemn them to operate referentially as statements about the state of sculptural realism itself.

But I suggest that, to the contrary, it is Mueck's realism that carries greater potential for facilitating an aesthetic politics in Rancière's sense. In particular, I propose that through their entrenchment in the museum context, Mueck's sculptures are exceptionally well situated for exploding the myth of metalanguage by replicating at the level of their form the metalinguistic function that, by virtue of their position in an art gallery, guarantees their artifice. Through their external framing as objects of art in a museum, Mueck's figures engage in a repetition of the same function (the confirmation of artifice) that they achieve at the level of form through their distortions of scale. Mueck's work thus points to an avenue for undermining the privilege that metalanguage enjoys within the representative regime, which diverges from the path suggested by *Love Soup* in which such repetition is absent. The confirmation of artifice that is established contextually amplifies the formal deception operating within Mueck's work. This puts into play a new twist on conventional trompe l'oeil. In particular, it allows the "seeing through" of the work's artifice at the level of form to resonate at a metalinguistic level. Furthermore, Mueck's work threatens the distinction between representation and the represented as well as between the true and the false. In short, by doubling the message conferred by metalanguage—the guarantee of artifice—within the form itself, Mueck's work compromises metalanguage's power to distinguish between truth and falsity and thus unsettles the foundation of our reality. Jenkins's work, by contrast, paradoxically consolidates the power of metalanguage by operating outside of the regulatory context of art.

In acting as its own metadiscourse on the institution of art, Jenkins's work ultimately leaves spectators on solid ground. Mueck's work, by contrast, points us toward a new distribution of the sensible that characterizes Rancière's vision for an aesthetic politics. But Mueck's work operates within the aesthetic regime of art, not through a break with realism but instead through an exploitation of the mimetic form's internal contradictions that, I have argued, render questions of truth and falsity indeterminate. It is here, rather than in its ability to convey hidden truths, where the rich potential for realism to contribute to a visual politics lies.

CHAPTER 2
Documentary Real-ism

Catfish *and* This Is Not a Film

This chapter explores two recent documentary films, one of which may not be a documentary, the other of which may not be a film. Although starkly different in their subject matter and political stakes, both *Catfish* (Ariel Schulman and Henry Joost, 2010) and *This Is Not a Film* (Jafar Panahi and Mojtaba Mirtahmasb, 2011) point to underappreciated dimensions of filmic realism, in particular its propensity to evoke what I will call "Real-ism" —that is, hints of the Real that emerge precisely when the symbolic framework governing reality becomes imperiled. Drawing furthermore upon Jacques Lacan's notion of the Real and Jacques Rancière's concept of the "aesthetic regime," I suggest that elements of conventional filmic realism have the potential to produce a politically destabilizing Real-ism, which, rather than involving the representation of reality in any recognizable form, calls forth that which is necessarily excluded/repressed from the symbolic framework.

For Rancière, the representative regime of art presumes a stable correspondence between a "type of subject matter and a form of expression," between the "the visible" and the "sayable," such as we find in conventional realism.[1] But Rancière emphasizes that, contrary to expectation, it is not necessary to abandon realism in order to break with the representative regime. Against the traditional interpretation, Rancière asserts that "the break with [the representational regime] does not consist in painting white squares rather than ... warriors."[2] What is required, instead, is giving up the opposition between reality and appearance that is essential to the representational logic.

Consequently, Rancière rejects a traditional politics of the image that seeks to inspire viewers to action by presenting them with realist representations of injustice. Rather than "counter-pose reality to its appearances," a Rancièrean aesthetic politics works "to construct different realities, different forms of common sense."[3] In other words, he advocates for a political aesthetics that emerges through the creation of a "dissensus" —a "reconfiguring of the distribution of sensible which defines the common of a community."[4] This disrupts established distributions of the sensible by severing expected correlations between images and their meanings and effects, forms of expression and their subject matter, and between "artistic hierarchies and social hierarchies."[5] The political force of such an "aesthetic regime" emanates from its ability to upset the naturalized, taken-for-granted system of perception that, by masking the exclusions upon which the impression of such a totality depends, perpetuates the illusion of total inclusivity. Thus, the political project put forth by Rancière does not merely seek to give voice and representational privilege to those who have been marginalized within a given system but instead requires challenging the very configurations of the sensible through which they have been excluded.

Of the two films under examination here, one appears to have no explicit political agenda (*Catfish*), and the other appears to embrace a politics of the image squarely in line with the representative regime (*This Is Not a Film*). But I argue, against expectation, both films activate the political potential that characterizes the aesthetic regime of art. Thus, the films point not only toward a tendency for the cinematic symbolic system to assimilate potential disruptions but also to a countervailing capacity of film to mobilize this very tendency in the service of "undermining" the given symbolic system. In arguing this, I draw upon Slavoj Žižek's insight that symbolic fictions operate "in one and the same move . . . [to] . . . bring about the 'loss of reality' and provide the only possible access to reality."[6]

CATFISH

Catfish, promoted as a "reality thriller," takes deception as its key topic of investigation. The film traces Nev (Yaniv) Schulman, a twenty-four-year-old New York photographer, throughout his year-long embroilment with a Michigan family. At the film's start, Nev has received a painting in the mail from an eight-year-old girl named Abby Pierce, who uses Nev's photographs of dancers as models for her own art. A correspondence develops between Nev and Abby's family, which spans a range of communication technologies from snail mail and cell phones to facebook and G-Chat (conspicuously devoid of its video potential). This leads to a romantic relationship between Nev and Abby's older sister, Megan, conducted solely over these communication devices. As Nev's feelings for Megan appear to intensify, so, too, do doubts that she might not be the person that she claims. Nev and the filmmakers (his brother, Rel [Ariel] Schuman, and friend, Henry Joost) set out on a trip to Michigan to investigate their suspicions that Megan and her family may not be who they appear.

At the level of content, uncovering the deception surrounding the identity of Megan and members of the Pierce family serves as the film's central narrative device. But through their quest to seek out the truth about the Pierce family, Nev and the filmmakers are suspected of perpetuating a hoax of their own. Specifically through the very act of making the film, Nev and his cohorts invite the ticklish question of whether they have indeed been deceived or whether, instead, they have deceived the audience about their deception. This suspicion is borne primarily out of what, in many of their comments, viewers have taken to be a flimsy initial premise for undertaking the documentary (a premise that Nev diegetically announces): to document Nev's budding long-distance correspondence with a promising eight-year-old painter, Abby. Viewer doubt about this premise circulates not around a concern that the film is unreliable in its presentation of the events, but rather around the fact of their presentation in the first place. As one reviewer puts it, "At what point would any filmmaker say "oh you know what, my brother got some paintings of his portraits from an 8 year old, that are mediocre at best, perhaps we should start documenting this?" [7] In short, the documentary's very possibility, it seems, hinges on foreknowledge of the twists that, in the film, take Nev and the filmmakers by surprise, a foreknowledge that contradicts the film's premise.

The editor of the *Jezebel* website encapsulates this view by explaining that the story of the Pierce family that the film documents

> is all real. But what critics have questioned is the authenticity of Nev's feelings for the fictional Megan, suggesting that he—along with Ariel and Henry—knew all along that the profile was fake, and that he was never really in love with Megan, but rather, led her on in order to make a better film.[8]

Movie-Line reviewer Kyle Buchanan makes the point more bluntly: "I think the filmmakers knew from the start what they had on their hands, and they baited a mentally unwell woman for almost a year until their film needed a climax." In sum, what appears to be at issue for most commentators is not the question of whether the events filmed are real, but rather whether the "feelings" that motivate the unfolding of the events are real.

Also fueling doubts regarding the film's credibility as a documentary is an implicit assumption regarding which of the different players in the film are most likely to be the tricksters and which the tricked. When asked to account for why audiences doubt the veracity of the documentary, Nev himself articulates the source of their doubt: "How could some country bumpkin in Michigan fool three savvy creative New Yorkers?"[9] Another reviewer is boggled by the thought that "three smart, tech-savvy New York hipsters could have been so easily misled. It certainly seems possible that they realized early on that Abby and her family were not what they seemed, and played along because it would make for a more interesting movie. This raises some thorny ethical issues, because if they did encourage the ruse, then the filmmakers are the cynical manipulators."[10]

I will suggest that Angela's (Abby's mother) response to being exposed as the perpetuator of a deception complicates the assumption that she has been exploited by the filmmakers, an assumption that, I will argue, operates to conceal ways in which Angela counters efforts to make her a passive spectacle. I contend that through disrupting this assumption, Angela introduces a dissensus in the film. In particular, she troubles the representative regime's efforts to categorize her merely as an object of interest, and she pushes the film into an aesthetic regime in which its excluded elements can become forceful disruptive agents.

For Rancière, the fact that *Catfish* demonstrates no explicit commitment to a political agenda is not a liability for its qualifying as a political work. Indeed, within a Rancièrian political aesthetics, the potential of images to affect a redistribution of the sensible rests merely "on [the] condition that their meaning or effect is not anticipated."[11] *Catfish*, I now argue, accomplishes this political feat by simultaneously exnominating (at the level of form) and giving voice (at the level of content) to bodies that are typically either (1) excluded from the dominant representational sphere; (2) included only to the extent that their inclusion is marked as exceptional; or (3) included as mere objects of scrutiny.

The deception (by Angela) that functions as the film's central narrative device begins to trickle over into the film's form when Nev and the filmmakers travel to Michigan in an effort to learn the truth about what they have come to suspect is an elaborate ruse. In the context of their burgeoning "virtual" romance, "Megan" sends Nev audio files of songs that she claims to have written and performed. Through a YouTube search, Nev discovers that these songs have already been recorded by a different singer. Soon a growing web of uncertainty entangles Megan's and Angela's claims to identity. This apparent revelation, we are shown, compels the Schulman brothers and Joost to embark on a disingenuous face-to-face encounter with the Pierce family, in which they seek to uncover the truth while concealing their suspicions.

The intersection of these two intradiegetic deceptions—the one of which Angela is suspected, the other by Nev and his crew—paves the way for a productive collision, which, I suggest, drives the film beyond the constraints of the representative regime. The men's intrigue surrounding the "truth" behind Nev's romantic entanglement (which teeters between giddy and sensationalist) meets the unexpected brute reality of Angela's life. We discover that she is a profoundly isolated, unfulfilled woman, largely responsible for the care of her two severely disabled step-sons (one of whom we learn has died by the time of the film's completion) and estranged from her older daughter, Megan—the template for the ersatz Megan, through which Angela forged the connection with Nev. An eight-year-old girl named Abby is indeed her daughter, but she is not the child protégé who painted the pieces sent to Nev; they are the work of Angela herself. Angela reveals an additionally disturbing detail—that she is about to begin chemotherapy for her newly diagnosed uterine cancer (a condition, we are told in the closing credits, that she does not have).

This presentation of multifarious layers of deception on the same representational plane facilitates a shift from the representative regime to the aesthetic regime of representation, and thus, from Rancière's point of view, constitutes a site of the film's radical political work. In particular, by refusing to adjust its filmic register to "appropriately" accommodate the pathos of Angela's life, the film performs a gesture central to the aesthetic regime: the refusal of the "presupposition that . . . some subjects are suitable for artistic representation while others are not . . . [and] that a series of changes can be made which render the inappropriate subject appropriate."[12]

From a Rancièrian perspective, there is an additional aspect of the film that may function in the service of an aesthetics politics. For Rancière, the exclusion of subjects from the sphere of "who counts" —whose existence is made "visible and audible within a particular aesthetic-political regime" — constitutes the key problem of political representation.[13] Aesthetics, the realm governing conditions and relations of visibility, is particularly well suited for disturbing established arrangements of who counts. In particular, by bringing into presence the bodies that fall outside the established bounds of representation, it counters the invisibility of the bodies whose exclusion lends a false sense of symbolic cohesion. Thus, it not only effects a redistribution of the sensible but also "introduce[s] into [our sense of community] new subjects and objects . . . render[s] visible what had not been, and . . . make[s] heard as speakers those who had been perceived as mere noisy animals."¹⁴ *Catfish* illustrates this Rancièrian politics by confronting viewers with an unsettling heterogeneity: Nev's exhilarating quest for the truth and the dreary bleakness of Angela's existence appear on the same representational plane. In this way, *Catfish* facilitates "a breakdown of the system of representation, that is to say, of a system where the dignity of the subject matter dictated the dignity of the genres of representation."¹⁵

In other words, *Catfish* disrupts the established distribution of the sensible by refusing to recognize the distinction it makes between objects, people, and events which can be appropriately accommodated into its image-repertoire and those which should be excluded in order for the representational system to appear complete and without contradiction. *Catfish* accomplishes this disruption by committing to an aesthetic regime that incorporates a principle of radical equality that makes it possible for everything to be represented: here "everything is now on the same level. . . . Everything is equal, equally representable."¹⁶ In particular, *Catfish* makes the radical democratic move of including Angela and her family within the realm of those "who count," along with the intradiegetically located filmmakers.

Indeed, Angela, in a sense, hijacks the film as a forum for her self-representation, thus achieving equality within the field of representation simply by enacting it. The film implicitly recognizes Angela's agency in making this radical move. In a keenly insightful soliloquy, delivered by Angela's previously reticent husband, Vince, we discover that the film is named for Angela. She is the eponymous *Catfish*, who in Vince's characterization "keeps people on their toes." Vince draws the analogy from cod exporters' solution to their fish becoming flabby and inactive upon arrival from long-distance shipments. Adding a catfish into the barrel, he tells us, keeps the cod lively and alert.¹⁷

Some viewers criticize Angela for not appearing ashamed at having masterminded an elaborate plan to fabricate her identity. Through the use of two cellphones, a phony Facebook account with make-believe Facebook "friends" (whose images she appropriated primarily from sites of people she did not know), and the adoption of a breathy voice (when impersonating "Megan"), Angela single-handedly created an entire network of family and friends as a scaffold for her "relationship" with Nev. And when confronted about her ruse, she seems to be more proud than ashamed for having kept the whole deception afloat. Indeed, her "confession" seems like a proud revelation of a magician who is finally at liberty to reveal her trick. Viewers' expression of distaste at this lack of contrition affirms the conventional representational regime that marginalizes Angela's agency against the film's radical strategy of giving her actions and motives (however "improper") "equal" weight.[18]

The impulse by viewers to distinguish Angela (and her family) as "improper subjects" within the representational system of the documentary takes a second reverse form. As I indicated earlier, rather than indict Angela for her seeming lack of remorse, many viewers and critics express concern that Angela has been unfairly exploited by Nev and the filmmakers. The filmmakers are frequently accused of having taken advantage of Angela's misery for the purposes of getting a good story. I suggest that both of these moves—painting Angela and her family as victims and criticizing Angela as an unrepentant conniver—work toward the same end. Both interpretations are implicit attempts, on behalf of the representative regime, to wrest the film away from the aesthetic regime by denying Angela the position of "one who counts." By contrast, along Rancièrian lines, the film eschews such conventionally prescribed interpretative and affective correlations by taking the radical political stance of refusing to judge Angela (through either the diegetic content or formal filmic conventions).[19]

THE REAL AND THE UNREPRESENTABLE

Let us now situate the question of how *Catfish* operates within an aesthetic regime of representation in terms of the context of a relationship between the conceptual frameworks of Rancière and Lacan. Rancière uses the term "heterology" to refer "to the way in which the meaningful fabric of the sensible is disturbed [when] a spectacle does not fit within the sensible framework."[20] But, as with the Lacanian Real, we should avoid being misled into thinking of such a "spectacle" as an external phenomenon that is too disturbing to be represented. In this respect we can consider an unsettling scene from *Catfish* in which one of Angela's nonverbal step-sons, impatient for her to stop talking with Nev so that she can prepare his lunch, is shown intently trailing her while carrying a cooking pot. This episode constitutes a Rancièrian disturbance, not because it is somehow inherently unrepresentable, but rather through the film's refusal to frame it as an unexpected "special" event that needs to be treated with a certain delicacy. That is, for Rancière, what is significant is not an element that is somehow intrinsically unrepresentable, but rather a perceived mismatch between the mode of representation and the subject it represents. The "spectacle," thus, can be understood as an artifact of the constraints that govern the representational system. Similarly, for Lacan, the Real emerges through the failure of the symbolic fiction to fully and without remainder represent the "whole of 'reality.'" Thus, by contrast with frequent characterizations of it as a terrifying Thing that causes the symbolic to warp in its attempts to capture it, the Real is not the external cause of stumbles in the symbolic system. Rather, as Žižek emphasizes, the Real emerges as the *effect* of the inevitable failure of the symbolic to flawlessly render reality fully and without remainder.[21]

In accord with these remarks, Rancière expresses "a certain intolerance for an inflated use of the notion" of unrepresentability.[22] "The assertion of unrepresentability," he argues, is a "claim that some things can only be represented in a certain type of form ... appropriate to their exceptionality. ... This idea [of unrepresentability] is vacuous."[23] In short, he dismisses the "impossibility of representation" as no more than a failure of the established representative regime to make an event intelligible. Such failures, he then argues, do not occur within what he calls an "aesthetic regime" because within this regime there is no presumed correspondence between making "visible" and making "intelligible."[24] Thus, the aesthetic regime embraces a principle of heterology, which, by making visible what is "unintelligible," opens up the possibility for new forms of thought and new realities to emerge.

Rancière's critique of the unrepresentable can be understood from a deeper metaphysical perspective. Reality as we know it hangs together on the condition that we avoid confronting the necessary exclusions which confer upon it an air of completion. As Žižek puts it, "the 'whole' of reality cannot be perceived/accepted as reality, so the price we have to pay for 'normally' situating ourselves within reality is that something should be foreclosed from it."[25] To prevent recognition of symbolic incompletion, the representative regime conspires to paint these necessary exclusions—what Lacan calls the Real—not as points of a fundamental failures on the part of the symbolic order but rather as markers of the "incapacity on the part of art" to justly render the full affective dimension of special events/moments/traumas. The Real, then, appears as art's incapacity to render the singularity of exceptional events intelligible.

In sum, paradoxically, it is through the philosophical conception that there are things which are "unrepresentable" that the representative regime consolidates a sense of symbolic wholeness. And this conception in turn masks the real/"Real" problem of representation: which is not that there are exceptional events (trauma, etc.) which fall outside of symbolic competence, but rather that the symbolic is constitutively unable to fully represent reality, full stop. The aesthetic regime, in effect, exposes this problem. By abandoning the expectation of an appropriate correspondence between exhibition and signification, it helps reveal that the problem is not that "language for conveying [traumatic events] does not exist," but much more disturbingly, that "the language that conveys the experience is in no way specific to it."[26] The obscenity, thus, lies in the fact that the existence of limits to an established system of representation is not due to exceptional, "unrepresentable" cases, but instead calls for some other "aesthetic" mode of expression. By insisting that nothing is unrepresentable and by representing everything on the same plane (for example, by refusing to make "adjustments" to more sensitively register the magnitude of an event), the problem of representation emerges as a problem intrinsic to the symbolic system itself, rather than a special challenge posed by exceptional "external" events. In Rancière's terms, there are no "events and situations which are excluded *in principle* from the adequate connection of a process of exhibition and a process of signification."[27]

We now seem to face what appears to be a contradiction between Lacan and Rancière, namely Lacan's insistence that the Real is intrinsically unrepresentable and Rancière's rejection of the idea of the unrepresentable. One way in which these two competing views may be reconciled is to emphasize that the Real—the failure of the symbolic system—cannot be represented within the representative regime, but that the representative regime's very failure to cope with the Real may be "activated" or indexed as an impossibility or absence within the aesthetic regime. Through the example of Claude Lanzmann's *Shoah*, Rancière makes exactly this point. In particular, he illuminates how what is unrepresentable in the representational regime may be displayed through the aesthetic regime. Rancière contends that the key representational challenge regarding the Holocaust lies not in

> reconstructing a gas chamber and its victims, but in the fact that we possess almost exclusively the words of a small number of survivors to inform us about a process conducted in secret. In the case of Lanzmann, there is a specifically artistic choice which is to activate absence—an absence of the things in the words, an absence of traces in the sites—so as to make the process of the double disappearance felt, by disconnecting it from any embodiment of external causality.[28]

Here unrepresentability emerges not as an ontological property of a horrific event, but rather as an epistemological contingency. Unrepresentability, in this epistemological sense, may be expressed through the aesthetic regime's capacity to evoke what exceeds the capacity of being shown within the representative regime. To be specific, within the aesthetic regime, dominant modes of perception are reconfigured in order to introduce the possibility of thinking something that was previously unthought. When an exceptional event occurs that causes the given perceptual system to stumble, the aesthetic regime's way of expressing this event is to make this upset palpable—to allow the disruption to be felt as a challenge to the given organizational system of perception, rather than dismiss it as unrepresentable. The aesthetic regime enables such challenges to produce heterologies within the realm of the perceptible, which make untenable the given order of sensible relations and incite the assembly of new distributions of the sensible.

Such a move, I will argue in the next section, is brilliantly facilitated in *This Is Not a Film*, in which Panahi cleverly expresses the impossibility of representing his treatment by the oppressive Iranian government. His representational challenge is doubled: he is both banned from representing (through the injunction to not make films) and prevented from being represented (through the prohibition to speak to the media). The film deftly accomplishes the expression of this double condition of unrepresentability not by merely making his circumstances visible, but rather by throwing into crisis the very representational system under which his plight is made invisible. Panahi thus employs the position of the double exclusion from which he speaks to highlight the double exclusion at the heart of the representational regime's "separation between the idea of fiction and that of lies."[29] In particular, I contend that by demonstrating, simultaneously, the impossibility of realism to draw out the truth and the necessity of fiction as a guise for arousing the Real, Panahi prompts a challenge to the very sensible system from which he is excluded.

THIS IS NOT A FILM

Whereas in *Catfish* the fact of the film's making figures retrospectively to imperil its documentary status, Jafar Panahi's *This Is Not a Film* takes the very fact of the film's making as the film's explicit subject matter. In the film, the internationally acclaimed Iranian filmmaker Panahi resourcefully attempts to represent his censorship by the repressive Iranian government. As a punishment for beginning to make a film that did not have government approval, Panahi was sentenced to a harsh twenty-year ban on making films, as well as put under house arrest, with an impending six-year prison term, and prohibited from leaving the country and talking with the media. This injunction rendered Panahi both unrepresentable and unable to represent, a point to which we shall later return. His response, *This Is Not a Film*, owes its international distribution to the successful smuggling of a USB drive baked into a cake shipped from Iran to Cannes, and received by allies from within the international film community. It is a film that cannot be a film without incurring further serious consequences.[30]

The film takes as its premise Panahi's impossible feat of making a film about his not making films. The opening scene of the film is shot with a stationary video camera positioned to face Panahi's breakfast table. Carrying a basket of bread, Panahi enters into the mise en scene, where he sits alone in front of the camera and begins to eat. While eating, he makes a phone call to invite his friend Mojtaba Mirtahmasb, a documentary filmmaker, to come over to discuss an idea. Upon his arrival, Mirtahmasb takes the reins of the camera as Panahi reveals his plan: because he is not permitted to make a film, he will have Mirtahmasb film *him* while he simply describes— "tells" —the film that he had begun when the injunction was imposed. Panahi compounds the duplicity evinced by the mismatch between the title of his film and its filmic status, through interdiegetic reminders that the contrivance of addressing the camera puts him in the position of what he describes as a "liar." Despite these protestations that the film is not only untruthful, but also "not a film," what unfolds on the screen is widely deemed as totally real.

One reviewer describes it as "one of cinema's rare masterpieces of truth."[31] Panahi's assertions that he is both not making a documentary and that he is lying do not imperil the film's realist status, but rather enhance it. When viewed as protestations triggered by Panahi's real circumstances, the very act of undermining the credibility of the project works to make it more credible.

A lesson from André Bazin helps us illuminate this phenomenon. Ivonne Margulies highlights Bazin's observations that cinematic images bear the "marks of two heterogeneous realities, the filmmaking process and the filmed event. . . . [T]he registered clash of different material orders best defines for him, in turn, that which is specifically cinematic. . . . What interests Bazin are precisely . . . the moment of encounter and productive maladjustment between representation and the actuality of filmmaking."[32] In this view, the cinematic essence for Bazin lies not simply in the camera's ability to indexically record reality, but rather in bringing these two dimensions into confrontation. Serge Daney cites Bazin's explication of this phenomenon: "'When a savage headhunter is shown in the foreground watching for the arrival of the whites, this necessarily implies that he is not a savage because he has not cut the cameraman's head off.'"[33]

This Is Not a Film highlights such "productive maladjustment" to powerful effect. The very titular announcement that what we are watching is "not a film" operates not merely as a metalinguistic comment regarding the nature of the object it describes, but rather works to draw attention to the impossible constraint under which Panahi labors. Thus, instead of wielding metalanguage as a tool for circumscribing meaning, the film's title functions to disperse meaning by operating as a prominent reminder of its conditions of production. In other words, the title does not simply stand outside and authoritatively comment upon the film, but rather enters into the intradiegetic struggles that the film recounts. In a similar way to the intradiegetic censorship matrix in *Love Soup* (discussed in Chapter 1), here, the film demonstrates the destabilizing effect that occurs when such acts of enunciation enter into the enounced content. In particular, we see how the very act of enunciation (the act of naming the film, *This Is Not a Film*) unsettles the truth value of the enounced statement (that this is, indeed, not a film). In this sense, I will also argue, *This Is Not a Film* differs from conventional realist films, which elide the disruptive potential of metalanguage by appealing to its transparent role of seamlessly complementing the content it designates.

THE REAL OF FICTION

Let us return briefly to *Catfish*, which I will argue provides a sort of counterpoint against which to analyze *This Is Not a Film*. Despite the filmmakers' resolute reassurances that the film "is 100 percent authentic, and all the footage is completely real and it's sequential and nothing was manipulated or staged,"[34] *Catfish* is widely considered to be a "fake documentary" —or in Morgan Spurlock's backhandedly effusive praise, "'the best fake documentary I've ever seen.'"[35] What is most significant, for our purposes here, is that many commentators who avow the film's fictional status hold this view alongside a belief in Nev's reassurances to the contrary. As I indicated, their doubt emerges, not from distrust that what they are seeing on the screen really happened, but rather from disbelieving the filmmakers' claim not to have suspected in advance what the film reveals. Against the standard view that indexical fidelity to profilmic reality secures a reality effect, here we encounter a phenomenon that demonstrates that the indexical tie to reality is not only insufficient for filmic realism but also may work to loosen its grip. In preparation for further the analysis of *This Is Not a Film*, I explain this phenomenon through an exploration of how, in *Catfish*, the mode of representation enters into the field it seeks to represent.

Catfish operates within what Bill Nichols calls the "reflexive documentary" mode, in which "we now see or hear the filmmaker ... engage in a meta-commentary ... about the process of representation itself."[36] *Catfish* includes recurrent diegetic references to the filmmaking process that take a range of forms, from Nev simply checking with the filmmakers to make sure that they can hear him, to arguments between Nev and his brother about Nev's frustrations with being continually filmed. For Nichols, this mode of metacommentary troubles a film's "assimilation by the conventions of realism" and raises the question of "its own status and that of documentary in general."[37]

The filmmakers of *Catfish* couple this reflexive approach with a commitment, at other times, to an "observational documentary" mode, in which the camera operates as an unobtrusive recorder of events. The combination of these two incongruous modalities impedes the film's ability to seamlessly function in either form. On the one hand, the film functions as a reflexive documentary, capable of "prompt[ing] the viewer to heightened consciousness of his or her relationship to the text and of the text's problematic relationship to that which it represents."[38]

On the other hand, this function is compromised by the film's adherence to the observational mode's perpetuation of the impression that the reality the film reveals is simply unfolding without intervention. By overtly intervening in the events that they seek to document, the filmmakers eschew a key documentary tenet—the construction of the impression that the profilmic events unfold independently of the camera's presence. As Rebecca Milzoff observes, *Catfish* eschews the expository documentary conventions of "talking heads or voice-over and doesn't include after-the-fact commentary—its action simply unspools like a scripted film's."[39]

This appropriation of the form of fiction undermines its realist status but, at the same time, I now suggest, enhances its potential for evoking the Real.

I have argued that the filmmakers employ an "observational documentary" approach in simply letting events unfold. Yet, rather than unruly spontaneity, the story that emerges follows an uncannily tight and dramatic narrative arc, rare in unscripted films. When questioned about this, the filmmakers cede creative credit to Nev's inherently "cinematic" life. Rel Schulman accounts for the film's surprising ability to both include everything relevant (even before the events to come could have been anticipated) by explaining that the "events in [Nev's] life are . . . so cinematic . . . and I've missed too many of them. So I just film him constantly.'"[40] This explanation points toward the Lacanian insight regarding the fictional status of reality itself. Žižek puts this insight in the following terms:

> if our social reality itself is sustained by a symbolic fiction . . ., then the ultimate achievement of film art is not to recreate reality within the narrative fiction, to seduce us into (mis)taking a fiction for reality, but, on the contrary to make us discern the fictional aspect of reality itself, to experience reality itself as a fiction.[41]

Žižek's point helps us to see through the real trap that the film sets for its viewers: the enticement to ask whether we are misidentifying a fiction as reality. Once we are released from this absorbing question, a more radical question may impose itself: is reality itself a fiction? In this way, the more crucial issue raised by *Catfish* is not whether it is realist, but rather whether it lures out the Lacanian Real.

FICTION OF THE REAL

For many other critics, the realist potential of *Catfish* is compromised not by a failure of indexicality, but rather by an excess: the fact that *Catfish* leaves us with no gaps. As one critic emphasizes, "In CATFISH, absolutely anything that holds any weight in the movie is on camera somehow. So [in addition to] running a production company and making another film at the same time as CATFISH they still had time to film Nev almost completely nonstop and at all the perfect moments. So this is either extremely lucky, or really staged."[42] Thus, rather than constant documentation working to ensure realism, metafilmic knowledge of how unlikely it is to capture everything (and in acceptable quality) imperils the film's claim to realism.[43]

A further analogy with Bazinian realism deepens this point. Bazin, as we have seen, points out that "narrative ellipses," omissions within a filmic text that occur in moments when the filmmaker would be in danger, strengthen the realist impact of a film. Ellipses mark the conspicuous intrusion of the filmmaking process into the filmed event with the effect of strengthening, rather than undermining, the film's claims to realism. In reference to Bazin's commentary on Thor Heyerdahl's *Kontiki* (1951), Philip Rosen asserts, "Here Bazin claims that realism is manifested by the film precisely because, at the moment when the filmmakers are depicted as being in danger, a chunk of time encompassing the events of most interest must be omitted. . . . This frustration acts to draw a greater quotient of belief from the spectator, for the interruption serves as evidence that the danger was real."[44] This recognition illuminates the ways in which conventional approaches to realism, built upon the premise of seeking to make the filmmaking process invisible through continuity editing, may actually make a film vulnerable to the breakdown of reality associated with the Real. Bluntly put: when filming headhunters, if the cameraman's head is not cut off, then the events must not be real; if the cameraman's head *is* cut off, then the event becomes Real. Thus, rather than pledge an unwavering commitment to the realist powers of indexicality and the erasure of the presence of the camera, certain profilmic events call for the switching off of the camera as an effective technique for accomplishing filmic realism.

Narrative ellipsis, thus, emerges as a precarious technique; it wagers that the destruction of transparent realism through the reminder of the camera's presence is more than compensated for by the creation of evidentiary realism. But this evidentiary realism hinges not on the camera's ability to impassively document the events in its purview; rather, it seeks to prove that the camera *was* really there, because it was affected by the very conditions it sought to merely record.

But here we encounter a point of divergence between Bazin's claim that, in certain instances of danger, intrusions of the filmmaking process into the filmed reality enhance a film's reality effect, and the way that, in *This Is Not a Film*, the intrusion of the filmmaking process into a dangerous filmed reality destabilizes claims to conventional realism—indeed provide the film with a link to the Lacanian Real. How might we account for this divergence? I suggest that there are two aspects of Panahi's film which lead the camera's intradiegetic involvement to disrupt conventional realism. First, by contrast with Bazin's examples, in Panahi's film, the camera functions from the start as an explicit diegetic object. The selection of which recording devices should be used (I-Phone or video camera) and the complex discussions that emerge over who should wield them play an overt role within the film. An awareness of the camera's presence is thus built into the content in such a way that it denaturalizes its role at the level of form, enabling it to accrue the power to unsettle conventional realism. Second, Panahi undertakes an ingenious two-part strategy for unsettling realism by (1) adhering faithfully—perhaps to the point of "overconforming," in Žižek's sense—to its most prized tenets, while (2) demonstrating the impotence of the realist form to render the truth. I develop these points in the next section.

SHOW AND TELL

Under the gaze of the camera, dutifully wielded by Mirtahmasb, Panahi's attempt at "telling the film," which he had planned to make, fails. His elaborate descriptions (replete with scenic demarcations, blocking, character descriptions, plot developments, etc.) come to an abrupt halt when Panahi, overcome by the futility of the endeavor, laments: "If we could tell a film, then why make a film?" I suggest that we read Panahi's remark as an insight into the necessity of deception for the emergence of the truth—a view akin to Žižek's stance that "in the guise of fiction, the truth ... is articulated."[45] The documentary form does not pave the path to truth; only fiction can provide "the protective mask" necessary for truth to emerge. In the particular instance of *This Is Not a Film*, Panahi demonstrates this viewpoint by explicitly performing the defiant act of making a film while proclaiming that he is not making a film. This act is further complicated by his claim that even when he explicitly makes films, he is not fully the maker—rather, his films contain moments of truth that escape his control. It is only when he is *not* making films that his films, in their full sense, are made. He thus effectively destroys the director function, from which he has been politically excluded, though the introduction of the paradox that his true moments as a director occur when he is divested of directorial authority—when an actor wrests control from him.

It is significant that Panahi does not simply *tell* us about this phenomenon, but rather *shows* us videotapes of his fictional films where his directorial authority is usurped by unanticipated intrusions of the Real. Through these clips, Panahi presents to us stirring instances where actors exceed their fictional assignment by recalcitrantly "speaking back" —either explicitly (as in the case of the child actor who tore off her costume—including an arm cast—because she had had enough) or more subtly (as in the case of an "amateur" actor who becomes so upset at his character's predicament that his organic expressions of agony begin to appear excessive for his character). Taken in and of themselves, these moments do not have the power to blur the boundary between truth and fiction. Rather, it is Panahi's aesthetic choice to include them, unremarked, within the completed film, that triggers such a blurring. Typically, if such scenes are shared with viewers, they are safely relegated to the circumscribed category of "out-takes," "bloopers," or "behind-the-scenes" footage. Marking the footage as exceptional thus reinforces the status quo. But, in these other films (of which he includes clips in *This Is Not a Film*) the exnominated inclusion of such unexpected moments has a destabilizing function.

In *This Is Not a Film*, Panahi adopts yet another strategy that undermines traditional realism. He includes unplanned, exceptional events and surprising filmic objects but marks them as such. For example, during Panahi's confinement in his house, he is asked to look after a veritable menagerie of animals (including his daughter's endearing pet iguana) and makes an extended acquaintanceship with the building's fill-in garbage collector. But rather than having these unexpected subjects appear in the film in the same register as Panahi himself, their appearances are marked as exceptional. The review of the film in *Time Out London*, for example, promises, "You haven't seen a scenery-chewing, scene-stealing supporting role until you've seen Igi, Panahi's four-foot long iguana, slithering diva-like into shot."[46] Most explicit in this context is the filmic treatment of the garbage collector, who inquires as to why Panahi is filming him on his I-Phone when a higher quality video camera is sitting unused in his living room. At this prompt, Panahi abandons the rhetorical device that he employs throughout the film up to this point: the conceit that if he is neither directing nor professionally filming the action then he is not making a film. He takes up the directorial reins by filming with the video camera and thus overtly marks the garbage collector/art student (as we come to learn) as a filmic object. The garbage collector's place in the representational scheme moves from a potentially disruptive inclusion (a person who typically falls out of the symbolic frame) to a circumscribed filmic object.

Despite this aberration, however, Panahi avoids taking up the role of the filmmaker through a double denial: both on the technical grounds that he is not making the film and on the philosophical grounds (articulated via his discussion of his other films) that his films are only ever really made when he is not making them. Panahi, thus, speaks from the only position from which his exclusion can be included. His dilemma cannot be represented through the representative regime, because the very ability to depict his double unrepresentability undermines his unrepresentable status. Rather, he cleverly succeeds in expressing the inability to both represent and be represented by "activating" a similar structural impasse through the ability of the aesthetic regime to evince a coalescence of being unrepresentable and unable to represent.

It might still appear that *This Is Not a Film* remains within the representational mode, apparently committed to traditional politics of the sort Rancière criticizes, in which images serve political ends through their ability to reveal to viewers a problem and consequently inspire them to take up action. But I suggest to the contrary that this very appearance contributes to the film's ability to facilitate a Rancièrian aesthetic politics. Panahi's passionate plea that he needs to "make" films, rather than simply "tell" them, lends the impression that he is committed to the constraints of the representational regime in which showing and telling function as distinct representational mechanisms, necessary for the appropriate rendering of specific events and objects.

This guise of matching a representational mode to represented event provides the occasion for the more radical assertion that, as an aesthetic form capable of luring out the Real, "making" (fiction) is preferable to "telling" (documentary). By adhering faithfully to the constraints of the representative regime—perhaps to the point of overconforming to its requirements, as witnessed through Panahi's emotional tribute to preservation of the distinction between showing and telling—Panahi establishes a foundation well primed for the injection of the Real. To be specific, by adhering to a stable model of exhibition and meaning in order to provide viewers with an ingenious code for undermining this very principle, Panahi succeeds in blowing apart the representative regime's logic from within the regime itself.

We may say that, through offering the examples of his own fiction films, Panahi provides us with a cunning cipher for his documentary, craftily pointing us toward the realization that fiction is necessary for accessing truth. In particular, Panahi's expression of feeling false when "playing" himself resonates with Žižek's description of how fiction is more successful than documentary as an aesthetic mode for luring the real: "When we film 'real-life' scenes in a documentary way, we get people playing themselves . . . the only way to depict people beneath their protective mask . . . is, paradoxically, to make them directly play a role."[47]

Panahi's commitment to fiction as the modality best suited to give rise to the Real is shared by Rancière. Thus, Rancière's claim that "the real must be fictionalized in order to be thought" should not be interpreted in terms of the postmodernist polemic that there is nothing real.[48] This assertion, rather, speaks to the Baudrillardian phenomenon in which the realms of fact and fiction become blurred through the ability of the simulation to precede, and hence organize, what we take to be reality. Fiction, here, can best be understood as the organizational schema for making reality both meaningful and coherent. Here Rancière shares Lacan's view that fiction and reality exist on the same side of the ledger, but he unites them in opposition to the Real. For Lacan, because reality itself is a cover for the Real, it requires a symbolic fiction for sustenance. Because the impression of an opposition between reality and fiction operates to mask their collusion, once the conspiracy between reality and fiction is revealed, the recognition of the fictional nature of reality yields to eruptions of the Real.

THE REAL/REAL-ISM OF LEAVING THE CAMERA ON

In quite distinct ways, *Catfish* and *This Is Not a Film* adhere to the importance of "leaving the cameras on" as a documentary tenet. For the filmmakers of *Catfish*, this act becomes crucial, not only as a principle informing their filming (for example, Rel's contention that that he must continually film his brother so as not to miss out on any moments of his reliably "cinematic" life) but also as a retrospective justification for the film's truth status in the face of its improbable premise. Yet, as I have suggested, rather than vindicate the film from accusations of fabrication, the claim to always have the camera on fuels these attacks. Although *Catfish* includes overt gestures to the filmmaking process within the film, the filmmakers' extradiegetic reassurances imply a false view of the camera as a neutral apparatus that mechanically records events within its audio-visual range; the filmmakers' disingenuous attempt to obscure their creative role merely casts a cloud of suspicion over the film. Thus, even if we accept that the events depicted did in fact occur without manipulation, the film's truth value is imperiled. In short, the execution of indexical fidelity is not sufficient for guaranteeing a film's truth status. Indeed, it seems that the reverse is true: by showing too much, by not missing out on anything, the reality effect is compromised.

Thus, *Catfish* points to another instance of the fruitfulness of Bazin's insistence on thinking of realism as a relationship between the filmmaking process and the filmed event. But rather than a "productive *mismatch*" between these two realms, we encounter a surprising *harmony* between them. Tom Conley describes how narrative expectations can be disrupted through the ability of the "passive register of the camera [to] dislocate the artistic privilege that a creator had owned when he or she was said to ... impose a 'vision' upon a form."[49] But in *Catfish* both the camera and the profilmic reality conform *too perfectly* to expected aesthetic conventions, creating an uncanny confluence that gestures toward the way in which reality itself assumes the form of fiction.

But perhaps the film's unsettled status as a documentary lends *Catfish* its principal tie to the Real. The refusal of the film to seal its generic status activates a productive indeterminacy that beckons the Real. The suspension of symbolic closure opens the path toward new configurations of the sensible in which truth and fiction are no longer counterparts, but rather co-conspirators in the effort to keep the Real at bay. Once their complicity is exposed, their efficacy in maintaining a taken-for-granted sense of reality is diminished.

In *This Is Not a Film* the commitment to leaving the camera on may be seen, in Jon Frosch's words, as nothing short of "an inherently political act of defiance."[50] Frosch reminds us that this position is held by Mirtahmasb himself, who tells Panahi, "What matters is that this is documented. It matters that these cameras stay on." This view appears to emerge from an anti-Rancèrian conviction that art becomes political through the creation of an "'awareness' of the state of the world."[51] Against this view, Rancière argues that political art must not merely depict a given state of events, but activate a "rupture" within the conventional logic through which these events are made meaningful.

But perhaps these two views of the political are not as far apart as they might appear. Documentation of a singular reality does not preclude its ability to rupture the dominant order of the sensible. Here we return again to Bazin, this time to his well-known example from "Death Every Afternoon," in which he confronts the disturbing ability of film to reproduce the singular event of death: "On the screen the toreador dies everyday."[52] Here, a singular reality takes on a sense of unreality through its impossible repetition. Cinema's initial ability to "record" an unrepeatable event works to secure its special status as a technology of the real, but its potential for incessant duplication ruptures its reality effect. Perhaps, then, Bazin's insistence that realism emerges from the relationship between the filmmaking process and the filmed event should be extended to include consideration of the viewing process.

Through the repetition of such singular moments, filmic realism may give way to Lacanian Real-ism. Fragments of reality begin to speak in new ways when assembled and reproduced within a cinematic context. Miriam Hansen credits Sigfried Kracauer with this insight in his famous late ode to cinematic realism, *Theory of Film: The Redemption of Physical Reality*. Hansen refutes the usual interpretation of Kracauer as a "naïve realist," insisting that for Kracauer, "cinema's photographic dimension emphasizes film's capacity to displace the world it depicts."[53] George Kouvaros cites Hansen's elaboration of this point in her foreword to *Theory of Film*:

> the same indexicality that allows photographic film to record and figure the world also inscribes the image with moments of temporality and contingency that disfigures the representation. If Kracauer seeks to ground his film aesthetics in the medium of photography, it is because photographic representation has the perplexing ability not only to resemble the world it depicts but also to render it strange, to destroy habitual fictions of self-identity and familiarity.[54]

In a similar vein, I suggest that the commitment to leaving the cameras on, for both *Catfish* and *This Is Not a Film*, undermines their claims to traditional realism but pushes them in the direction of the Lacanian Real. The potential for these films to destabilize the given distribution of the sensible is enhanced through their use of the documentary form to highlight the fictional nature of reality itself. By drawing attention to the illusion of completion that undergirds our symbolic system, these films enable new configurations of the sensible to emerge and therefore help us to envision a "world . . . in which everyone counts."[55]

CHAPTER 3

An Uncertain Indeterminacy

Aliza Shvarts's Unseen Senior Project

In April 2008, Yale University senior Aliza Shvarts made international headlines when reports circulated that her senior-year art project involved documenting a nine-month cycle in which she repeatedly inseminated herself while taking herbs to induce a miscarriage. Her project, which was cut from the university's senior show amid controversy (and has never to date been exhibited), consisted of projecting video footage documenting her bleeding in her bathroom onto a cube draped in blood-stained sheets. Although the media dubbed her piece "abortion art," Shvartz maintained that the crux of the piece lay in rendering ambiguous, for both herself and her viewers, whether she had become pregnant and miscarried or whether the blood was the result of menstruation.

In Yale University's official response to the controversy, spokesperson Helaine Klasky described Shvartz's project as a piece of "performance art" and a "creative fiction"—designations used to imply that Shvartz's acts were not "real." Klasky also reported that Shvartz had admitted to several Yale administrators that "she neither impregnated herself nor induced any miscarriages"—a statement interpreted by media reports as an acknowledgment of a hoax. When asked to comment on this revelation, Shvartz characterized Klasky's testimony as "ultimately inaccurate," maintaining that she did indeed carry out the procedures that the piece documents, although she left the outcome of the acts uncertain.[1]

Customarily, an institution's admission that a documentary art piece under its auspices was a hoax would be an embarrassing, if not credibility-breaching, disclosure. Yet in the Shvartz case such a declaration was made to augment rather than impeach the institution's integrity. To further complicate matters, Shvartz bristled at the allegations of a hoax, asserting, "I'm not going to absolve them by saying it was some sort of hoax when it wasn't. . . . I started out with the University on board with what I was doing, and because of the media frenzy they've been trying to dissociate with me."[2] In another twist, Klasky responded to Shvartz's reply by announcing that Shvartz had "vowed that if the University revealed her admission," she would deny it. Her denial was part of her performance: "We are disappointed that she would deliberately lie to the press in the name of art."[3]

At first blush such rhetorical gymnastics appear to invoke the logic of a "double deception," in which a subject lies "by telling the truth." According to Jacques Lacan, only humans are able to "pretend to pretend. . . . [An animal] does not make tracks whose deception lies in the fact that they will be taken as false, while in fact being true ones, ones, that is, that indicate his true trail."[4] In double deception we expect that what we are told or shown is a lie, so if it turns out that we have been given the truth, we feel lied to—doubly deceived. This is what Slavoj Žižek refers to as telling the "truth in the guise of a lie."[5] Žižek, following Lacan, argues that such acts, which "imitate the dissimulation of reality," carry disruptive potential by facilitating an unexpected confrontation with the truth when one is confidently expecting fiction.

I argue that Shvartz's performance falls short of creating a double deception and can be more suitably understood as a bungled attempt at staging a simulation. As a result, I contend that not only does her work fail to act as a socially disruptive force but that it also provides institutions geared toward upholding order with an opportunity to strengthen their repressive grip. This chapter uses Shvartz's case as an occasion to assess the political implications of artistic forms in which claims of layered deception play a central role. Specifically, the Shvartz controversy enables us to focus on the respective difficulties encountered in both dissimulation and simulation as strategies for upsetting the social order.

The controversy surrounding Shvartz's project differs from more familiar controversies surrounding video documentary, which tend to center on the truth claims of documentary forms of representation. We commonly encounter accusations that a video "lies" by representing fiction in the form of fact—a form of deception that follows the straightforward logic of the fake. But in Shvartz's case, no one questions whether the events displayed in the video—Shvartz's bleeding in her bathroom—really occurred. Rather than trying to fool us into mistaking fiction for fact, Shvartz encourages us to experience facts as if they are no more than fictions. Such a strategy, Žižek suggests, carries subversive potential if it succeeds in upsetting the fantasy framework upon which reality depends. Shvartz's case, by contrast, reveals the way in which this strategy can also be deployed in the service of a conservative form of postmodern thought.

In such cases a mere epistemological uncertainty, such as our inability to know whether Shvartz became pregnant and miscarried, gets mistaken for an ontological indeterminacy. Going beyond a blurring of the distinction between truth and falsity, such an error creates the impression that there is no real event to be known and, as such, reduces reality retrospectively to a discursive artifact.

We can see this mistake at work in Shvartz's rhetoric. She boasts that "no one can say with 100% certainty that anything in the piece did or did not happen."[6] But she then confuses epistemology with ontology by adopting Jean Baudrillard's language of the simulation. For example, she explains in the *Yale Daily News* that "the piece only exists in the telling. This telling can take textual, visual, spatial, temporal and performative forms—copies of copies of which there are no originals." Here, she slides from a claim about the inability to know what happened to a claim that nothing exists that can be known. Her confusion points to a key tension within the political potential of simulation as a transgressive form of deception. Simulation, in its proper form, presents us with the ontological puzzle of indeterminacy. By disrupting the symbolic order—or, in Baudrillard's terms, the "principles of reality"—such a form has transgressive political potential. Its potentially disruptive nature is often marked by responses of institutions of power to reframe them as examples of mere uncertainty.[7] But this is definitely not the same as the postmodern "relativist" approach that sacrifices reality altogether in favor of discursive effects.

In the context of this distinction, we see that the radical political potential of Shvartz's piece is sacrificed on the altar of postmodern erasure of reality in favor of discourse. To be specific, rather than actually producing a simulacral piece, Shvartz merely fakes it. Her claim to have created a simulation is itself a dissimulation—a contention that reveals the implicitly reactionary nature of the project, despite the subversive political potential suggested by her rhetoric. I further argue that in faking a simulation, Shvartz not only falls short of undermining the principles of reality but also provides institutions of power and order with opportunities to more firmly stake their claims. This difficulty guides us toward a more general difficulty with the use of simulation for eroding the reality principle upon which law and order thrive.

As Baudrillard's example of a "simulated hold up" (discussed in Chapter 1) makes clear, the difficulty of staging a proper simulation is compounded by the pragmatic glitch: if it is successful, it will be mistaken for reality. Institutions of power will also work to deny its status as a simulation. A "real hold up," Baudrillard argues, "only upsets the order of things . . . whereas a simulated hold up interferes with the very principle of reality."[8] Thus, a simulated crime poses a much greater disturbance to law and order than does a real crime. A real crime emerges as an aberration that reinforces existing law and order, whereas a simulated crime "suggests . . . that law and order themselves might really be nothing more than a simulation."[9]

As a result, when faced with a simulation, holders of power "always opt for the real," by working to "reinject realness and referentiality everywhere, in order to convince us of the reality of the social."[10] Brian Massumi echoes this point that systems of power benefit more from pushing the simulation in the direction of reality than by denouncing it as a fake. He asserts that "the best weapon against the simulacrum is not to unmask it as a false copy, but to force it to be a true copy, thereby resubmitting it to representation and the mastery of the model."[11] This move works to prevent the indeterminacy produced by a simulation from posing a challenge to the "reality principle." Such challenges confront us with glimpses of what Lacan calls the Real, the dimension in which the symbolic order, through which reality is sustained, shows its cracks.

This connection between Baudrillard's concept of simulation and Lacan's notion of the Real helps to foreground why a true simulation is both so potentially subversive and so difficult to achieve. For Lacan, the Real points to limitations within the sociosymbolic order that violate the consistency of what we think of as reality. Such anomalies must be covered over by the symbolic system in order for what we perceive as reality to make sense. Because it defies symbolization, the Real can never be fully apprehended, only glimpsed through unsettling missed encounters. To be specific, eruptions of the Real disturb our sense of reality by confronting us with phenomena that, more than uncertain, are indeterminate. Their disruptive potential lies in such indeterminacy that defies systems of classification. In the words of Paul Verhaeghe, these disturbances "can no longer be put into words. . . . This dimension beyond the signifier is the Lacanian real."[12]

True simulations can exist, I contend, only within this realm of the Lacanian Real. In the other two registers posited by Lacan, the Imaginary (which facilitates identifications through appearance) and the Symbolic (which structures the world through systems of signification), simulation is impossible. In these realms we can ever only dissimulate. I learned this all too well while in college when, for a period, I was preoccupied with trying to look taller than I really was. My first attempt at faking a tall appearance was a disaster. I wore pants that were a bit too short, applying the logic that if I really was a tall person, then it would be difficult to find pants long enough to suit my limbs. Therefore, I reasoned, even if I did not "appear" tall, any thinking person would deduce that I must nonetheless actually "be" tall. The visual effect was, of course, that I actually looked shorter, because the foreshortened pant legs created the appearance of even squatter legs. Because it relied upon cultural knowledge and inference, this was an attempt at dissimulation at the level of the symbolic.

After catching sight of myself in a full-length mirror, I soon realized the ineffectuality of this strategy of symbolic deception and took my dissimulation to the level of the imaginary. This involved the more obvious but opposite approach of wearing pants that were a bit too long, creating the illusion of longer legs. Yet this approach also failed, because anyone who really thought about it would know that pants appear too long only on people who are too short. In sum, it seemed the only option was the impossible prospect of creating indeterminacy about my height that would throw into crisis the very categories of short and tall. Such a radical undermining could take place only through simulation in the realm of the Real, the difficulty of which I was unable to negotiate.

Despite its attempt to enter the transgressive realm of simulation, Shvartz's piece, like my own misguided dissimulation of height, fails to move beyond the status of a dissimulation. Yale University's insistence that Shvartz had confirmed that her piece was a "creative fiction" (or, in the mass media's terminology, a hoax) and that she therefore had not become pregnant precisely enacts the move that instruments of power would be expected to make when faced with a threat to the existing order—namely, attempting to diffuse the threat by assimilating it into the symbolic order, thereby reinstituting the binary logic of true and false that is characteristic of dissimulation. By substituting uncertainty for indeterminacy, Shvartz herself unintentionally appropriates this tactic in which conservative forces defuse simulations. To be specific, she ambiguates the question of the piece's truth or falsity by stating that "no one can say with 100% certainty that anything in the piece did or did not happen."[13] She thus creates mere epistemological uncertainty rather than the full-blooded indeterminacy required for simulation to occur. In sum, despite her implicit invocation of Baudrillard, Shvartz misses the mark in creating a simulation. Instead, as I did with my strategy of wearing pants that were too short in order to fake a taller stature, she does no better than achieve a dissimulation in the symbolic realm.

CODA

In a later reflection upon the controversy, Shvartz incisively identifies the clash between the dominant institutional framework of the University and the counterhegemonic goals of art activism as a site not only of limitation and restraint but also as a necessary and vital tension for provoking unexpected shifts in perception. As Rancière has emphasized, a political work of art cannot aim to trigger a particular outcome, but it can, at best, create new ways of thinking that undermine governing hierarchies of perception. Shvartz herself can be seen as advocating such a reading of the political possibilities of art when it performs what she calls "figuration and failure": a viscerally charged and affectively disturbing engagement with bodies in the act of failing to conform to symbolic, aesthetic, and institutional expectations.

Reconsidering her senior-year art project in different terms, Shvartz tells us: "There is something cruel in the fact that the activist pedagogical practice with which I identified and in which I attempted to participate existed in the same institution as the pedagogies my work targeted. ... I have [now] come to conclude that this type of cruelty is the ... true pedagogical imperative ... to reform from the inside, to split, counter, upheave, and upset."[14] Shvartz, here, points not merely to some unfortunate conjuncture in her own case, but, I suggest, to a more general limitation in the usual conceptualization of "activist" art. Here, we encounter the recognition of the political possibilities that emerge from the "cruel" impossibility of stepping outside of the institutions that one critiques. Shvartz's comments point toward the Rancièrian position of aesthetic politics, in which rather than seek to critically comment on an institution—"with the wish to explain and mobilize"—one offers a view from within an institution which enables new connections to be made and offers the potential for its governing framework of meaning to "explode."[15]

The piece planned by Shvartz may have come close to producing the "double effect" that, for Rancière, characterizes "suitable political art": "the readability of a political signification and a sensible or perceptual shock caused, conversely, by the uncanny, by that which resists signification."[16] But, I maintain, her piece—in its purely discursive context—falls short on both sides. The piece fails both to articulate a "readable" political message and to instill a rupture of the sensible. On the first score, the spectacle she stages readily feeds both a dominant perceptual framework and repressive institutional forces; on the second score, the possible irruption of the uncanny into the sensible order is reduced from the disruptively indeterminate to the merely epistemologically uncertain. Indeed, one might argue, ironically, that it was the move by Yale University to pull the piece from the senior show that opens up the transgressive possibilities associated with the Lacanian Real. To be specific, by remaining absent and unseen—a gap in the symbolic—Shvartz's piece finally threatens to become not merely uncertain but rather truly indeterminate.

CHAPTER 4

A Ruse for the Real

Christoph Schlingensief's Deportation Installation

Traditional liberal notions of democracy, which emphasize deliberative reason and consensus building, paradoxically end up creating exclusions. This is the view of many social theorists who recognize that although liberal democracy appears to incorporate all difference of opinion, it in fact creates consensus only at the cost of rendering invisible what is deemed excessive. This chapter follows this line of thought in seeking not only to expose the invisible structure of exclusion at the core of liberal democracy but also to explore the role that art may play in terms of political possibilities of what has been termed a "radical democratic" approach to urban public space. I argue that "Bitte liebt Österreich," the controversial public art installation by the late German conceptual artist and political provocateur Christoph Schlingensief, challenges traditional democratic positions and opens up a space for a radical democratic project. Schlingensief's piece, I argue, contributes to radical democratic thought by demonstrating how democracy is strongest when it is understood as a process of continually disturbing the meaning and constitution of the social.

As a contribution to the Vienna International Festival in June 2000, Schlingensief erected a complex of two-story "containers," housing twelve people presented as asylum seekers, which he installed in the city's center. Surrounding the containers stood a metal fence, security guards, and surveillance cameras (which broadcasted events both inside and outside the containers on local monitors as well as on the Internet). On the outside, the containers bore a variety of provocative signifiers, including, most prominently, a large banner with the Nazi SS motto "Ausländer raus" ("foreigners out"), alongside flags from the FPÖ (a right-wing, nationalist party that in 1999, under the leadership of Jörg Haider, won 27 percent of the nation's votes in the general election).

Passersby and the 800,000 online followers of the event were asked to cast their vote each night for which two detainees should be sent back to their countries of origin. In addition to a modest cash prize, arrangements would be made to provide the remaining detainee with legal residency through marriage to an Austrian citizen—volunteer permitting. At the conclusion of the weeklong event, the artist and immigration activists reminded the crowd that at this very moment millions of asylum seekers are being detained in actual containers at airports throughout Europe, awaiting deportation.

Schlingensief's piece prompts consideration of Rancière's view of aesthetic politics as the basis of "democracy." The installation/performance, I argue, succeeds in "interrupting the distribution of the sensible by supplementing it with those who have no part in the perceptual coordinates of the community, thereby modifying the very aesthetico-political field of possibility," which, for Rancière, characterizes democracy.[1] In what follows, I will flesh out the nature of the political intervention accomplished by this piece, with an emphasis on its relationship to realism and deception.

Staging his exhibit as a "game" that borrowed from a familiar media genre of reality TV enabled Schlingensief to articulate a social reality with unparalleled clarity. It also enabled him to fulfill Georg Lukács's progressive political project of exposing the "hidden and contradictory" nature of that reality.[2] More than that, I shall argue, Schlingensief's exhibit invites us to consider the following novel possibility: that using a fictional, game-like, mode of representation to describe a politically *reactionary* event may help to subvert it.

In other words, I will argue that Schlingensief's project not only fulfills the Lukácsian demand for a "progressive realist" fiction which "de-reifies" or "de-naturalizes" reality but also accomplishes the more radical possibility of undermining a conservative state of affairs, by highlighting what Slavoj Žižek describes as the "fictional aspect of reality itself."[3] The lure Schlingensief uses to entice us is, on the one hand, benignly familiar (a silly reality TV show) and, on the other, ominously strange, thus setting a ripe scene for exposing the artificial frameworks through which reality is represented. To think in Žižek's terms, Schlingensief provides us with an opportunity to encounter Truth where we presumed to find 'mere appearance': the 'shock of the truth' consists in its sudden emergence in the midst of the realm of reassuring phenomena."[4] From Žižek's point of view, such cases can be said to exemplify Jacques Lacan's premise that Truth emerges in the guise of a lie.

As such, they contrast with traditional realist representational modes that use fictional forms in order to communicate revolutionary content, and which may be said to "lie in the guise of the truth." As Lukács puts it, fictional forms which employ "documentary procedures [...] end up by fetishizing facts;" they "lie" through the "confusion of the totality with a mere 'sum of facts.'"[5]

In such traditional realist texts, Lukács explains, "anything accidental is ruled out. Nothing comes about that is not prescribed by the plan."[6] And as such, Lukács argues, they neglect to pay proper attention to what he calls the "dialectical combination and inextricable coalescence of accident and necessity."[7]

Žižek makes a similar move in arguing that there are two modes in which ideology operates, and they privilege accident and necessity, respectively. Ideology is usually conceived in its first form, as a naturalizing device, which enables mere contingencies (national boundaries, for example) to appear necessary. Yet, according to Žižek, ideology also accomplishes the inverse function: it causes necessity to be perceived as mere contingency. Under this second mode of ideology, one dismisses as accidental the structural requirements of the system. In Schlingensief's exhibit, for example, the plight of asylum seekers appears as an unfortunate but anomalous situation. But this appearance obscures the ways in which the conditions that make life unbearable in the native countries of asylum seekers are imbricated in the prosperity and excesses of Western Europe and the United States, the deprivation of world resources by the West, and the requirements of the global market. What is thus dismissed as disruptions to the system's normal functioning turns out to be its hidden conditions of possibility.

According to Lukács, we can avoid traditional "regressive" modes of realist forms of representation through a "progressive" realism that incorporates a dialectical understanding of the ways that "accident and necessity" occasion one another. Such a progressive realism may be achieved through the "mechanical exaggeration of necessity" to the point that it "collapses into its opposite."[8] I suggest that "Bitte liebt Österreich" not only meets this dialectical challenge posed by Lukács but also disrupts *both* of the ideological modes to which Žižek draws our attention. In addition, as we will see, the piece fulfills Rancière's aspiration for an aesthetic politics by demonstrating the ways in which a dissensus functions to disrupt the usual organization of the intelligible.

Let us now consider how these two different frameworks help illuminate the political work that Schlingensief's piece performs. One of the aims of the piece, according to immigration activist Pete Galindo, was to demonstrate the contradiction between the unsympathetic rigidity that national borders pose to people and the generous permeability that they offer to "dollars and multinational corporations."[9] By, thus, "de-reifying" the concept of national borders, the exhibit disrupts ideology in its first form, its naturalizing mode, in which accidents are mistaken for necessity.

In addition, however, rather than dismiss reality television as an incidental amusement, Schlingensief draws connections among the seemingly disparate events of the global proliferation of reality TV, the plight of refugees, and neoliberal conditions, thereby helping us to see the "necessary' role it plays in securing contemporary social reality. As the deprivation of public space robs people of opportunities to fictionalize their own lives, mediated forms of intimacy step in to buffer the loss. Reality television's binding social function, much like the neurotic's symptom, not only *expresses* an underlying problem (in this case, neoliberalism) but also provides techniques for coping with it. As Laurie Ouellette observes, reality television not only substitutes for the loss of public life, but it also trains viewers to live with the deprivation of public support structures. Shows like *Big Brother*, she suggests, "construct templates for citizenship that complement the privatization of public life, the collapse of the welfare state, and most important, the discourse of individual choice and personal responsibility."[10] By embedding the struggle of asylum seekers within the mold of reality television, "Bitte liebt Österreich" invites us to recognize that not only are refugees casualties of neoliberal policies but also that citizens well schooled in neoliberal values (the very morality lessons taught by reality TV) are encouraged to see their plight as the result of a personal failure to fulfill neoliberalism's most foundational virtues, which Ouellette identifies as "self-sufficien[cy], responsib[ility], and risk-aver[sion]."[11] The public opinion of reality television as trivial amusement blinds us to its constitutive role in maintaining this neoliberal fiction. And conversely, I will argue, the role played by "Bitte liebt Österreich" in making us aware of this conservative political valence of reality television, disturbs ideology's second mode of operation, in which necessity is dismissed as mere accident.

The political intervention made by Schlingensief's project can be more fully appreciated by contextualizing it in terms of two other cultural artifacts from this period that contribute to debates surrounding multiethnic nationhood. Through examining these artifacts, we see how "Bitte liebt Österreich" points, in a novel way, to the friction between identity politics and a "melting pot" view of multicultural identity, a debate that gained renewed saliency in the German-speaking world in the early 1990s after the reunification of Germany.

The first of these cultural artifacts was an ad campaign designed by the international advertising agency Scholz & Friends to run in the German newspaper *Sächsische Zeitung* and on local billboards in an attempt to promote multiculturalist acceptance as a response to a surge in racist violence. One design featured a close-up of the face of a dark-skinned man with the caption, "Ein Sachse." For Mark Rectanus, the success of such an approach depends upon a "binary and assimilationist view of identity," in which one should be accepted on the basis that one *is* German rather than on the basis of ethnicity, race, and so on. In opposition to this liberalist logic, Rectanus proposes a more radical position—"the much more threatening notion that [one] should be accepted on the basis of *not* being German, for example, as a migrant or asylum seeker, whose legal status may be indeterminate."[12] The second cultural artifact is the cover of a 1993 special issue of *Time* magazine with the lead headline, "The New Face of America: How Immigrants Are Shaping the World's First Multicultural Society." The cover displays a computer-generated composite face of a "multiethnic" woman, synthesizing Anglo-Saxon, Middle Eastern, African, Asian, Southern European, and Hispanic physical characteristics. In Victor Burgin's assessment, "although only 15% Anglo-Saxon, the woman nevertheless has the appearance of a White woman recently returned from a holiday on the Mediterranean."[13] Here, although the question of legal national status is evaded (she is not an actual person after all), it seems that her Anglo appearance alone qualifies her for acceptance.

Together, these two artifacts embody the fantasmatic structure of two different visions of national identity. The *Time* magazine example illustrates the dream of a system lacking in contradiction, a "melting pot" vision that Burgin describes as "a democracy without differences, in which everyone could pass as a more or less legitimate child of the founding fathers."[14] This vision of symbolic unity rests upon what Burgin refers to as "a nostalgia for ignorance of lack and of loss, for a time before 'castration'"—where "castration" here is to be understood as a metaphor for the loss or lack that inevitably accompanies one's entry into the social world.[15]

The "Ein Sachse" example, by contrast, demonstrates the way in which the "ethnic other" comes to function in a world of difference. The anxiety of "castration" or loss is mitigated through the creation of "fetishes"—surrogates for what is perceived as missing. The apparent coherence of a system is constituted through the addition of what Žižek describes as "an excessive element which 'sutures' it precisely in so far as it sticks [. . .] out as an exception."[16] The conspicuously "other" other functions as the exceptional figure to whom the inconsistencies of the social world can be attributed and thus becomes necessary for sustaining an illusion of unity and sameness.

By contrast with "melting pot" depictions of multiethnicity, identity politics of the sort represented in the "Ein Sachse" ad campaign attempts to repoliticize difference, but it does so at the risk of essentializing race and ethnicity. By standing behind, and claiming as one's own, an identity designated by one's "dominators," one might successfully "reverse" its significance from a negative to a positive meaning. In doing so, however, one nevertheless reasserts the authority of the symbolic fiction to adjudicate which particular markers of "difference" are socially meaningful.

The limitations of these two artifacts suggest the need for a different approach to identity that could, for example, hold in tension the black Saxon's identity both as German and as a person of color living within a country where markers of racial difference structure both social phantasy and material relations. Something akin to this approach can be seen in Gayatri Spivak's notion of strategic essentialism: provisionally appropriating the oppressors' label in order to fight for rights on behalf of the oppressed group—with the understanding that any politics based on the categories of assigned identity must attempt to displace the ideological and fantasmatic structures that ground these very distinctions. The challenge of keeping these distinctions in play while avoiding the risk of essentialism involves what Colin MacCabe describes as the "refusal to discount any of the multiplicity of subject-positions which [one] has been assigned [as melting pot approaches require] or to fully accept any of them [as straightforward identity politics demands]."[17]

MacCabe's charge nicely encompasses the challenge that Schlingensief's piece prompts. But I follow Stuart Hall in refusing to locate this disruptive play within the reaches of strategic essentialism. Strategic essentialism, for Hall, fails to account for the full and ambiguous expression of hybrid identities—identity positions that cannot be, even for strategic purposes, made into pure categories. Furthermore, for Hall such a position fails to do justice to the constitutive nature of representation—the ways in which representation does not simply convey existing identities, but rather intervenes in the very process of how identities come to be formed, expressed, and understood.

I suggest that, in refusing to view the social as a liberal democratic sphere for which the goal is merely the assimilation of additional bodies and identities into its established structure, "Bitte liebt Österreich" overcomes the limitations identified by Hall. It does so by pointing to a radical democratic sphere in which the illusion of inclusion depends on the exclusion of bodies and identities that antagonize the given system. Schlingensief's work, thus, challenges the traditional democratic positions represented by *Sächsische Zeitung* and *Time* magazine and opens up a space for a radical democratic project in three ways: (1) it generates a space in which irrational passions are not only mobilized but also engaged; (2) through the appropriation of the *Big Brother* hook, it facilitates identification with the excluded other of liberal democratic systems (in this case, political refugees); and (3) the project carries ambiguity about whether it is meant to endorse or critique Austria's immigration politics, thus constituting an inviting space for "irreducible conflicts" to emerge. Thus, Schlingensief's piece fundamentally disrupted the possibility of consensus, because observers did not know where to stand in relation to it: those with similar viewpoints often found themselves at odds with one another, and those with opposite viewpoints and political orientations often found themselves in agreement. As Andreas Hudelist, citing Claire Bishop, describes, "Please Love Austria" demonstrates that "participatory art is not a privileged political medium, nor a ready-made solution to a society of the spectacle, but is as uncertain and precarious as democracy itself; neither are [sic] legitimated in advance but need continually to be performed and tested in every specific context."[18]

Beyond the issue of its political efficacy, Schlingensief's project raises vital questions regarding the use of art to intervene in the political sphere. Rather than attempt to detail the effects of artistic practice on politics, I follow Hall once again in asserting, as Rancière does, that art's (or for Hall, theory's[19]) power to intervene in politics is most potent when a space is created for allowing these two spheres to be held "in an ever irresolvable but permanent tension [...] [such a space] continuously allows the one to irritate, bother, and disturb the other, without insisting on some final theoretical closure."[20] This quotation holds special relevance here since it speaks to the very notions of antagonism and uncertainty that constitute the "hallmark[s]" of radical democracy and of Schlingensief's provocation.[21] Like the relationship between art and politics, democracy itself is strongest when it is understood as a process of aggravating the meaning of the social, rather than as a product of such negotiation.

CHAPTER 5

The Faux and the *Schmo*

Parodying Reality TV

Since Laura Mulvey (1975) posed the pivotal question of whether female spectators could avoid the patriarchal temptations prompted by the realist conventions of mainstream cinema, feminist film theorists have remained pessimistic about the potential for realist modes of representation to challenge cultural norms. For Mulvey, the gaze required by mainstream cinema is male. Under the male gaze, woman becomes the object of "fetishistic scopophilia," enabling the spectator to take pleasure from both viewing the woman's body and identifying with the male protagonist, all the while shielding himself from castration anxiety. In this view, the female spectator is sentenced to either give up the pleasure of viewing or take up one of two equally unsavory viewing positions: narcissism (through identifying too closely with the desired woman on-screen) or masochism (through taking on the masculine desire for the female sexual object).

Although this problem of female spectatorship is an old one, it has endured. The roots of its tenacity grow from its commitment to (1) an adherence to a model of ideology based primarily upon resistance; and (2) a model of the gaze based upon mastery rather than uncertainty. In this account, I seek to shift the terrain away from these assumptions and call, instead, for a view of a potentially subversive female spectatorship position that foregrounds the limitations of traditional ideology-critique and locates the gaze in the place we cannot see. In this way, I hope to restore the possibility of pleasure for the female spectator, without sentencing her to the two disappointing patriarchal viewing options that Mulvey entertains.

In particular, against Mulvey, and following Tania Modleski, I contend that "there must be *other options* for the female spectator than the two pithily described by B. Ruby Rich: 'to identify either with Marilyn Monroe or with the man behind me hitting the back of my seat with his knees.'"[1] The "other option" that I develop here involves rejecting both of the positions that Rich suggests. In particular, rather than dismissively indicting the fetishistic structure for upholding patriarchal formations, I suggest that it is precisely through exploiting the tensions gnawing the split at the heart of the fetishistic inversion, between "knowing very well" "but even so" acting to the contrary, that one can arrive at a subversive spectatorial position that avoids Mulvey's objections.

I argue for the possibility of this subversive viewing position by considering the American faux reality TV show *The Joe Schmo Show*, a program intended by its creators "to parody reality TV." In Chapter 4 we encountered a different sort of parody of reality television in the form of Christoph Schlingensief's "Please Love Austria." In the case of Schlingensief's piece, the neoliberalist premises of reality television are transferred into unexpected contexts—performance art and Europe's refugee crisis—where their political implications become stark. Schlingensief uses the reality television as what Doug Kellner refers to as a "dual optic": as not only a cultural form to be examined but also as a conceptual tool for shedding new light on the sociopolitical world within which it emerged. In the case of the *Joe Schmo Show* we encounter a parody of reality television of a different sort, one that is internal to the genre itself.

I suggest that *The Joe Schmo Show* promises a virtually irresistible viewing position of mastery, only to pull the ground out from underneath, leaving the spectator to flail among the contradictions that the position of mastery seeks to erase. Thus, rather than simply inverting the position of mastery and displacing it by one of ignorance and captivation, the viewing subject is left to inhabit the gaps between the two. Jacques Lacan associates this position with the "feminine masquerade." Such a position, I will argue, carries potential for a subversive feminist spectatorship.

Critical indictments of reality television often claim that it foments voyeuristic tendencies by enabling audiences to feel as if they are privy to the spontaneous unfolding of intimate moments. Barbara Creed, however, rejects this criticism by suggesting that "watching movies *per se* is a far more 'voyeuristic' act . . . [because] it hides its modes of production and pretends that the spectator is viewing unmediated reality."[2] *Big Brother*, according to Creed, through its overt generic structure and its potential for audience interaction (in the form of casting votes regarding which participant will be made to leave the house), "makes no such pretence" to transparency. For

Creed, not only does reality television free the spectator from voyeuristic entrapment, but it also works to "subvert the conventional ethnographic gaze in order to represent the dominant culture looking at itself 'warts and all.'"[3]

But does reality television work to facilitate this blunt confrontation with our flaws? Or has Creed fallen for the temptation against which she warns: seeing reality television as an unmediated and revealing engagement with our most intimate realities? Creed concedes that participants on reality television shows comport themselves, largely in accordance with the expectations of the genre. The radically unexpected action of Merlin Luck, a participant in Australia's 2004 *Big Brother* series, accentuates just how tightly the participants conform to implicit generic constraints. As Luck entered the audience-filled studio for his live-to-air "eviction" interview, he pulled out a banner bearing the words "FREE TH REFUGEES" (according to Alex Broun of the *Green Left Weekly*, the "E" fell off in his haste to unravel the sign) as well as a strip of wide black tape, with which he quickly sealed his mouth. His protest and silence resulted in audience jeers and his eventual removal from the studio by security guards. Luck, in effect, inverted the expectations of reality television by doing something truly unexpected.

Luck's intervention undermined the illusion of critical distance and related anonymous pleasure of voyeurism that is confidently offered to cynical viewers of reality television. But, I argue, it did so merely by encouraging viewers to discard one spectatorial position (the mastery of distance/voyeurism) in favor of another (the impotence of captivation/suture). To be specific, the power of Luck's protest depended precisely upon its inversion of the implicit, yet rigid, constraints of the genre—and by inverting them merely confirming them. By contrast, I shall argue that in *The Joe Schmo Show* the positions of distance and captivation remain perpetually provisional, their seductions serving as a persistent reminder of the impossibility of symbolic closure. Thus, although Creed is right to point to the subversive potential of reality television, in my view it is to *The Joe Schmo Show*, rather than to *Big Brother*, that we must look to find it.

But before considering *Joe Schmo*, let me set the scene. Early November 2003—the "sweeps" period for network television—three made-for-TV movies, *Saving Jessica Lynch* (NBC), *The Elizabeth Smart Story* (CBS), and *The Reagans*, garnered much press attention. Lynch was a nineteen-year-old supply clerk for the US Army, stationed in Iraq during the 2003 invasion. She was injured when her convoy took a wrong turn and was ambushed. Lynch was taken to an Iraqi hospital, where after eight days of being listed as a POW, a special force of the US army stormed the hospital to "rescue" her. Subsequent media reports suggest that the rescue mission, which the army filmed, was a publicity stunt, aimed to counter resistance to the war. As described by a doctor at the hospital who witnessed the scene: "It was like a Hollywood film. They cried 'go, go, go', with guns and blanks without bullets, blanks and the sound of explosions. They made a show for the American attack on the hospital—action movies like Sylvester Stallone or Jackie Chan."[4] The fictional nature of the filmed "attack" is evident in the well-documented fact that two days prior to the rescue, Lynch's doctor at the hospital had made arrangements for Lynch to be transported by ambulance to the US Army.

The subject of the second made-for-TV movie, Elizabeth Smart, was abducted in 2002 at the age of fourteen from her Utah home by a local indigent man who had once worked as a handyman for the Smart family. After being missing for nine months, the police discovered Smart (wearing a disguise), walking with her captor and his accomplice just several miles from her home. The two made-for-TV movies, *Saving Jessica Lynch* and *The Elizabeth Smart Story*, aired opposite each other days after the real-life Lynch and Smart each made the talk show circuit recounting their respective experiences of captivity and rescue. The sequence of these media events—real-life figures telling their own stories closely followed by movie versions of the same events—would seem to indicate that these teledramas embraced something other than a purely documentary function. Lynch's and Smart's televised appearances, it seemed clear, served as promotional devices for the dramatizations of their tales, each of which followed disclaimers reminding viewers that some of the events may have been created for dramatic purposes. The reminders reinforce the remark by NBC's head of movies and miniseries, Jeff Gaspin, that ratings have very little, if any, relation to a made-for-TV movie's truth claims. As Gaspin explains about an NBC program chronicling the rise and impending fall of Martha Stewart: "we still don't know what she did yet [regarding her indictment on financial misdoings] but it was a very compelling movie, a very highly rated movie, a very successful movie."[5]

Now consider the third made-for-TV movie, *The Reagans*, slated to air later the same November on CBS, amid enormous pressure from the political Right, who decried what they saw as an unflattering portrayal of the former president.[6] These protests would seem to presuppose the existence of viewers naïve enough to believe fictionalized narratives. I argue that, on the contrary, it is precisely the fact that viewers do *not* believe—that they "see through"—these representations, that validates the concerns of the detractors of *The Reagans*. Made-for-TV movies like *The Reagans*, *Saving Jessica Lynch*, and *The Elizabeth Smart Story* work by inviting viewers to distance themselves from the movies by taking up a position of mastery—of one who knows better. Such distance does not undermine ideology; rather it is a requirement for its smooth functioning. As Slavoj Žižek puts it, "the lesson is clear: an ideological identification exerts a true hold on us precisely when we maintain an awareness that we are not fully identical to it."[7] This, I claim, is how we should understand the protests by opponents of *The Reagans*. Their protests indicate their implicit and correct recognition of the Žižekian point that the acknowledged fictional nature of made-for-TV movies reinforces rather than weakens their ideological hold, and thus that "seeing through" a fiction implicates, rather than extricates, subjects from its ideological grip.

Perhaps rarely is the position of "seeing through" made simultaneously so inviting and yet so unsustainable than in another television show that received much attention in the period leading up to the November sweeps, Spike TV's (the station that boasts being "the first network for men") *The Joe Schmo Show*.[8] The show's premise rests upon a cast of actors fooling an earnest participant, Matt Gould, that he is involved in a *Big Brother*–style reality TV show. As Tom Keogh explains, *The Joe Schmo Show*'s premise:

> [it is] a real-life variation on the Jim Carrey comedy *The Truman Show*, in which Carrey played a man unaware he is the star of a television series, living on an enormous set and surrounded by actors playing family, co-workers, neighbors, etc. *Joe Schmo* fools a gregarious, likable 27-year-old fellow, Matt Kennedy Gould, into believing he's part of the cast of a reality-TV program called *Lap of Luxury*, competing for a $100,000 prize by surviving humiliating trials and those inevitable, once-per-week evictions of unlucky contestants.[9]

Safely scaffolded within this parodic framework, viewers of the show were both in on and yet safely distanced from the ruse. Rather than read parody as a form that undermines the ideological force of the text, for Žižek, such mechanisms (as parody, cynicism, irreverence, mockery, irony, etc.) strengthen viewers' ideological investment in the text. Ideology *depends upon* subjects' ability to distance themselves from it; thus, such seemingly nonconformist positions turn out to be the very requirements for making an ideology "workable." It is, conversely, an "overly literal" relationship to ideology that has the potential to make an ideology untenable, by collapsing the necessary distance between it and its subjects. In this chapter, I argue that *The Joe Schmo Show* escapes the reactionary function that, for Žižek, characterizes the parodic form.

Fans of *The Joe Schmo Show* admit a curious attachment to the show in spite, or perhaps because of, its contrivance. As one fan admits, echoing the structure of the fetishistic inversion: "even though we know its rigged, we still want to know the outcome ... even though I knew it was all planned out, I still got tense during the eviction ceremonies."[10] But, and here is the feature of this show that distinguishes it from other reality programs, including the made-for-TV movies that I mentioned: rather than try to disavow or explain away this contradictory experience, viewers take pleasure in it. They revel in the possibility that rather than occupying a position of mastery, they may very well turn out to be the dupes.

Viewers openly speculate on fan sites that a "twist ending" might reveal that Matt, the unsuspecting Joe Schmo, was in the know all along and has fooled both the hired actors and the viewers alike. These speculations indicate that Matt's rare earnestness and enormous attention to detail continually posed unforeseen challenges to the actors and viewers. For example, in an early episode showing the group's first dinner, Matt interrupts just as his housemates are about to take their first bite. It occurs to him that "Molly," a character who has introduced herself as a virgin with strong religious convictions, might like to say a blessing before they eat, an unexpected, though totally appropriate, comment which temporarily discommodes the actors. In the show's third episode, the eviction of his pal, "Earl," brought Matt to tears. Upon hearing the news he collapsed on the stairs in despair and sobbed into his hands that "no amount of money was worth this pain."[11] Could it really be possible that Matt has bought the premise so thoroughly? Or has he caught on and is turning the tables? Or is it the audience that is being gulled by an actor playing Matt following a scripted twist?

The case of *The Joe Schmo Show* seems to suggest a precariousness within parody. Through a series of hitches and gaffes, it tipped over into something more like trompe l'oeil, enticing viewers to play with their own implication in its ruses. But unlike traditional trompe l'oeil, in which what appears at first glance to be "real" turns out on closer inspection to be fake, in the case of *The Joe Schmo Show*, what viewers are convinced is mere artifice turns out to contain authenticity. As a result, the distance characteristic of the fetishistic inversion collapses.

With standard reality TV shows, by contrast, the fetishistic inversion remains firmly intact. As viewers, we know that reality TV is, in fact, a sham. Through a combination of casting decisions, generic conventions, celebrity aspirations, and so on, the participants of these shows are, in effect, not acting "authentically," but rather are "playing roles." Nevertheless, we enjoy watching them as if we think of them as "real people." This convention is mocked by *The Joe Schmo Show*'s planned inclusion of the familiar reality TV "characters" in their cast list: the "Virgin," the "Rich Bitch," "Dumb Jock," and even the "Smarmy Host," and so on, a mockery to which the audience is alerted intradiegetically. Nevertheless, as viewers, we enjoy watching them, as if they were "real people." As one fan explains on his web blog, this contrivance actually lends the show an air of authenticity: "To make this [ruse] seem authentic, the cast has specific parts to play which are satires of the types of people you tend to see on the Real Reality shows."[12] In short, in the case of *The Joe Schmo Show*, the producers explicitly expose the sham that we know reality TV to be, leaving us nothing to "see through." Thus, there is no fetishistic inversion; instead, we encounter a coincidence between what we "know" and how we "act."

It would seem to follow that, as viewers, our position with regard to Matt should be to align him with participants in standard reality TV shows. And because, as far as Matt knows, he is entering a standard reality TV show, we would expect him similarly to adhere to its generic expectations. But, like *Big Brother*'s Merlin Luck, Matt does not hold up his end of the bargain. The fetishistic inversion becomes untenable as a result of his (unintentionally) disruptive actions; Matt took the show's fake premise more sincerely than participants of actual reality TV shows do. Indeed, the show's co-creators, Rhett Reese and Paul Wernick, were so troubled by the depth of Matt's "investment in the show and the people around him" that, they tells us, "there were times we wanted to stop the show."[13] The show continued with the aid of a series of emergency meetings in which ideas were discussed for recalibrating the narrative in the light of Matt's unpredictable behavior. Thus, rather than sustaining the split between "knowing" and "acting," Matt's involvement in the show led to its suturing. Our "knowing" (that Matt is a reality TV participant like all the others) was troubled by Matt's "authenticity" to the point that it came into coincidence with our "acting" (as if we were indeed watching someone's genuine actions), thus canceling the fetishistic inversion.

I suggest that Matt's spontaneity functions in a more subversive way than Merlin Luck's overt attempt at subversion. Luck's intervention worked to secure our identity as spectators who cynically "see through" the pretense of reality TV. His act confirmed what we already knew: that reality TV could not accommodate a truly "real" act. Luck's unambiguous break from the reality TV show format leaves spectators without any uncertainty regarding their viewing position and, thus, reinforces spectators' confidence in seeing through the purported "realism" of reality TV.

This conclusion aligns with Rancière's position that an aesthetic political intervention cannot be undertaken with the intent of consciousness-raising and the mobilization of affect. As Rancière cautions, "political art cannot work in the simple form of a meaningful spectacle that would lead to an 'awareness' of the state of the world."[14] An aesthetic-political moment can emerge, rather, when something shifts the sensible framework within which meanings and hierarchies are disrupted.

It may not be solely that Matt's unexpected, nonconformist behavior is responsible for facilitating a shift in the given coordinates of the sensible, which put viewers' confident position of mastery in suspension. Matt also exhibited what viewers widely perceived as rare "sincerity." His display of having been seen to try to make "real," or "authentic," attachments and offer genuine reactions to contrived scenarios might hold the key to the disruptive nature of his performance. As mentioned earlier, following Baudrillard, reality television performs a "deterrence function" "by presenting us with a world that is obviously fake, we are distracted from recognizing the artificiality of the world itself."[15] The reality-affirming "deterrence function" depends upon the spectator encountering an obvious fiction, which allows for easy distinctions to be made between the fiction and their reality. Matt, I suggest, disrupts the deterrence function of reality television by failing to uphold our ability to adjudicate reality from fiction. If it is, indeed, the fictional context created by the producers of "Lap of Luxury" that enables Matt to be so "real," then perhaps our lives too require fictional support for reality to take shape.

A recent fictional television show, *UnREAL*, which has garnered somewhat surprising critical acclaim, enacts a parody of reality TV, which is similar to *The Joe Schmo Show*. By contrast with *Joe Schmo*, *UnREAL* avoids the contrivance of including an unsuspecting "real" person—a figure intended to embody the role of the "subject supposed to believe" (a position discussed in Chapter 1). But, like *The Lap of Luxury* (the fictional reality TV show at the center of *The Joe Schmo Show*) *UnREAL* claims to take us behind the scenes of a *Bachelor/ette*-style reality television show called "Everlasting." As Kevin Fallon points out, the premise of a fictional show that claims to pull back the curtain "on what goes into making a reality TV show ... [is] a brilliant conceit.... Reality TV was supposed to be the curtain-less medium, a voyeur's look into the lives of other people, unfiltered."[16] The artifice of *UnREAL* is lent some degree of credibility because it is frequently mentioned that the creator of the show, Rebecca Shapiro, is a reality television insider who was a producer of the actual *Bachelor/ette* programs for ten years. Some critics claim that the show's success comes from its ability to address a savvy viewer; simply highlighting the artifice of reality television is not enough, they argue, because viewers "more than ever ... are sophisticated enough to realize that they are watching a constructed narrative."[17] The achievement of *UnREAL*, then, seems to emerge from its ability to "truly hammer home the human cost of that [reality]," in particular, the ways in which racist and sexist assumptions are reinforced in order to accommodate expectations of what makes for good television.[18]

But, I suggest, as a critique of the genre, *UnREAL* too easily accommodates a viewer "in the know," a spectator who can watch comfortably as an unimplicated party. Indeed, this latest twist on the genre might turn out to fulfill a similar function to the genre's original architype, *An American Family* (1971–1973) featuring the Loud family. Both this first and this most recent incarnation of the genre may be seen as performing what Jean Baudrillard describes as a "deterrence function." By taking us behind the scenes of a "reality" that is revealed to be manipulated, viewers may be deterred from recognizing the ways in which their own "realities" also rely on fictional support.

TOWARD A FEMINIST SPECTATORSHIP

My analysis of *The Joe Schmo Show* facilitates a response to the key question posed by feminist film theory: What are the possibilities for a feminist spectatorship in the context of realist modes of representation? To develop my argument, I make three shifts. First, unlike much scholarship in this area, I suggest that we do not consider intradiegetic characters as examples of representations of men and women. Instead, I suggest that we focus on how a text may promote, in Jacques Lacan's terms, "sexuated" ways of looking.[19] In other words, I take the issue to be what it means to look *as* woman rather than *at* woman—a move away from thinking about how a woman *is looked at* (how she is *seen*) to thinking instead about how a woman *looks* (how she *sees* as woman.) In this sense, my project elucidates Jacqueline Rose's recommendation that feminist film theory must seek to elaborate "not just what we see, but how we see."[20]

This account involves a second shift—a move away from exploring the relationship of "reality TV" programs to notions of reality, in favor of discussing "reality TV's" relationship to the domain Lacan calls the Real—anxiety-provoking anomalies arising from the failure of the symbolic order to perfectly render reality. The Real marks the traumatic "nothing" around which the symbolic is structured. It is the job of what we think of as "reality" to protect us from the Real, by providing us with a symbolic framework that covers over the Real's disruptive effects.

The third shift entails moving away from a focus on "sex" and "gender" to a focus on Lacanian processes of "sexuation," through which subjects cope with the threat posed by the Real to their sense of identity. Sexuation, it is important to note, refers to woman and man not as biological categories (sex), nor as cultural overlays (gender), but rather to the two possible positions that a subject can take in response to the failure of the symbolic system to confer identity. In short, the sexes "male" and "female" mark the two logically possible ways in which the symbolic fails.

The key question then becomes whether a subject responds to this failure through the structure of what Lacan calls "masquerade" (the domain of woman) by exercising his or her libidinal economy around the active questioning of sexual identity. Or does the subject, instead, take up the position of "imposture" or "display" (the domain of man), by confirming his or her sexual identity through investing in the authority of the symbolic to act as a guarantor (i.e., shoring up all of "reality's" resources for blocking out the Real). A spectatorship position based upon the logic of "the feminine masquerade automatically poses a question [i.e., "who am I for the Other"], while masculine identification with law, logos, or authority tries to stop the question."[21] In particular, when viewers face a challenge to their comfortable position of mastery, the viewing strategy of man entails attempting to "refuse that moment ... by trying to run away from it or by binding it back into the logic and perfection of the [visual] system itself."[22] Such efforts yield reactionary results by attempting to reinscribe lack back into the symbolic order.

Reality television, in its usual incarnations, would seem to facilitate a spectatorship position based on the strategy of imposture. Viewers' investment in the "symbolic fiction" is rewarded by the pleasurable unfolding of predicable events. For example, by enabling us to "see through" smoothly the fictionalized scene, shows like *Saving Jessica Lynch*, *The Elizabeth Smart Story*, and *The Reagans* consolidate the viewer's own identity as one who knows, thus facilitating the spectatorship position of man.

A parody of the structure and rituals of reality television would seem particularly welcoming of this strategy. But, in the case of *The Joe Schmo Show*, we have seen, just as the viewers' position of mastery seems most certain, the symbolic fiction begins to falter. Yet, rather than try to ignore or cover over these disruptive moments, viewers relish the uncertainty. Here, then, we see a different viewing position emerging, namely the viewing position of woman, which undermines a symbolic system's coherence by inhabiting, rather than concealing, its points of lack and excess. In this sense, I argue that the Lacanian position of woman provides a structural model upon which a subversive viewing practice may be based. This spectatorial position involves identifying with the gaze, but in the Lacanian sense of the gaze, not in the sense that Mulvey invokes in referring to the male gaze. For Mulvey, "the male gaze" refers to the position of mastery through which viewers identify with the male protagonist and see the on-screen women as an erotic object that possesses what she calls a "to-be-looked-at-ness." For Lacan, by contrast, the gaze has nothing to do with mastery and possession. Indeed, as Elizabeth Cowie emphasizes, "the gaze is the inverse of the omnipotent look ... [it is what] surprises the subject in its desiring."[23] Thus, in Lacanian parlance, what is usually called the "male gaze" more precisely describes his notion of "the look." The gaze, for Lacan, resides, then, not on the side of the subject, but rather emanates from the object. It rouses us out of any complacent viewing position that seeks to master its object and instead confronts us with a fascinating uncertainty. Identification with the gaze, in this Lacanian sense, is associated with the position of woman.

A final irony now emerges: it appears that Spike TV, the "first network for men," has effectively positioned its viewers in the Lacanian position of woman. Indeed, the irony is doubled because, if I am right, then this viewing position carries the radical potential for which feminist critics, like Creed, have looked to the reality TV genre. But, it turns out (contra Creed), that this potential is located not in reality TV itself, but in its parody, a point which, in turn, challenges us to a reconsideration of Žižek's formulation of parody's reactionary function. My analysis here has taken up this challenge, using insights from Baudrillard and Rancière to expose radical possibilities inherent to parody.

CHAPTER 6

Corporeal Realism

Bodyworlds *and* Cloaca

Two art exhibitions concerning different sorts of "realist" representations of the human body set the scene for this chapter: *Bodyworlds*, Gunther Von Hagens's unprecedented public display of "plastinated" human corpses, and *Cloaca*, Wim Delvoye's mechanical and electronic installation replicating the functions of the human digestive system, from swallowing to elimination. One might imagine that *Bodyworlds*, an exhibit that encourages visitors to confront their "deathly doubles," would provoke horror and that a machine designed to eat and excrete would be regarded by viewers as little more than a novelty. However, accounts of the reception of these two installations reveal the unexpected. Media reports of visitors' responses to *Bodyworlds* indicate fascination but provide very few, if any, markers of a traumatic encounter. *Cloaca*, by contrast, seems to provoke a surprisingly disturbing effect among viewers. As one critic observed: "visitors walked out with a strange look on their faces, as if they'd just paid a visit to the devil. . . . At a school visit, a little girl burst into tears in front of the machine."[1]

I will suggest that although *Bodyworlds* was heralded in the media as a spectacle of "the living dead," it reveals instead a comforting fantasy of the dead living. Rather than confront us with the chilling realization that we are beings heading toward death, the "plastinates" uphold the ultimate symbolic fiction—that we can survive our own death. This comforting thought is expressed by comments made by people who have agreed to donate their bodies upon their death to Von Hagens's Institute for Plastination.[2] One donor, for example, describes his or her reason for choosing to be plastinated after death in these terms: "The thought of being buried in the earth after my death is a horrible one as far as I'm concerned, because I am completely disgusted by worms and grow panicky when I think of them. Now I can relax about the issue, though, since I can stay above ground after my death."[3] The donor here speaks about death not only as if he will live through it but also as if he will remain saddled by his earthly phobias—a frightening new twist on the persistence of the symptom. Von Hagens's corpses, in this sense, affirm a subjectivity insulated from intrusion by the Other.

Even for those, like myself, who did not take comfort in the exhibit, but rather found the display of corpses disturbing, I suggest that the exhibit nevertheless serves a self-protecting function. For Julia Kristeva, the corpse and dung occupy a special category of the abject: objects that "stand for the danger to identity that comes from without: the ego threatened by the non-ego, society threatened by its outside, life by death."[4] She places these in opposition to a second category of the abject associated with "the danger issuing from within the identity (social or sexual)," of which menstrual blood is paradigmatic.[5]

Within this first category of the abject as external danger, Kristeva makes a critical distinction between the corpse and dung as forms of the abject, by setting apart the corpse as the "utmost of abjection."[6] All other abject forms share a self-recuperative potential in that they, in Kristeva's words, "show me what I permanently thrust aside in order to live."[7] The expulsion of the abject object thus helps to guarantee the integrity of the subject who does the expelling. The corpse, by contrast, annihilates the border between "the place where I am not and which permits me to be"; it operates as a "border that has encroached upon everything . . . It is no longer I who expel, 'I' is expelled."[8]

But in comparing *Cloaca* and *Bodyworlds*, we encounter a reversal of Kristeva's expectations. Here, the seemingly entertaining dung-producing machine, *Cloaca*, functions more like the corpse does for Kristeva than the actual corpses used in *Bodyworlds*. Thus, *Bodyworlds* and *Cloaca* present us with two different forms of encounter between subject and object: whereas *Bodyworlds* presents us with the threat of the Other that lurks within, *Cloaca* confronts us with a more radically desubjectifizing encounter with the subject that lurks beyond. Or to put it in other terms, *Bodyworlds* presents us with the object in you, but *Cloaca* confronts us with the recognition that you are in the object.

MIMESIS, MIMICRY, AND MINIMAL DIFFERENCE

To develop this line of inquiry, we must first consider the ways in which the plastinated corpses and the shitting machine are like us—what representational forms and methods enable them to appear in some sense as our doubles? It seems that *Bodyworlds* presents us with a fairly straightforward case of mimetic realism—the plastinates look like us. They not only resemble us under our skin, but they also mimic our daily pastimes, from playing basketball to chess. For Jeremy Bentham, who had his own body preserved and displayed after his death, the preserved corpse is the ideal embodiment of the subject—constituting what he called an "auto-icon." As Miran Bozovic explains, for Bentham, "Since nothing resembles an individual as well as that individual represents him or himself, the bodies of the dead need to be preserved as their own most adequate representations."[9] *Cloaca*, by contrast, is characterized by an antimimetic form of realism—what we might call a functional realism. As Delvoye puts it, the "shocking thing is that it doesn't look like a human being. . . . It is like a wheel. The wheel isn't trying to look like your feet, but it does the same thing as . . . feet do."[10]

It would appear to follow that *Bodyworlds*'s mimetic realism, with its potential for blurring the boundaries between self and other, would bring the threat of death near to viewers. For Roger Callois, mimicry, in its strongest form, involves a "drive to indistinction."[11] But, Lacan argues, mimicry, as it pertains to animals in the natural world, should not be seen simply "in terms of adaptation" or self-preservation.[12] What should be emphasized in the case of an insect blending into its surrounding environment is its engagement in a self-annihilating practice—a giving up of the boundaries that separate the organism from the environment—the self from the other.[13] Denis Hollier complicates Callois's account of mimesis as a "threat to difference," by stressing that the insect "can only play dead because it is alive."[14] Lacan, too, highlights this significant dimension of mimicry in arguing that "mimicry reveals something in so far as it is distinct from what might be called an *itself* that is behind."[15] This position illuminates the way that "resemblance" and "identity" function as differential terms: because the plastinates exhibited in *Bodyworlds* resemble us, they must not *be* us—this palpable distinction reminds us not of our impending death, but rather of how very alive we are. "Mimesis," as Hollier puts it, "pretends to announce the end of differences . . . but only the better to preserve the vital difference."[16]

Bozovic contrasts this position to Bentham's concept of the auto-icon, in which a thing best resembles itself, by pointing out, "a thing does not look like itself"—it *is* itself." Here, as in Hollier's account, resemblance "guarantees Non-Identity," rather than identity. Indistinction, paradoxically, becomes a marker of difference, rather than sameness. At first sight, this move might seem analogous to the argument that mimicry functions as a self-protective mode, which Callois and Lacan reject. But a key difference separates Hollier's account from traditional arguments regarding the adaptive function of mimicry: for Hollier, the self-protection offered by indistinction is gained not through the denial of difference, but rather through the very assertion of difference.

An example from the sitcom *Seinfeld* helps us to see how this phenomenon works: Jerry's friend, George, often calls him for help when he gets into ridiculous predicaments that could *only* happen to George—that are quintessentially George (such as when he calls to ask Jerry to call in a bomb threat to his office in order to avoid being caught napping under his desk). As soon as Jerry answers the phone, George immediately blurts out his problem to which Jerry responds, with exaggerated mock-surprise, "Who is this?" This comical gesture engages with the psychoanalytic tenet of how a too-close resemblance confirms difference; when it could *only* ever be George, then of course it can't be George. The joke works by highlighting that when resemblance is too complete, we have encountered an excess—the *objet a*, which marks the thing that is "in you more than yourself."[17] This acknowledgment points to the fact that the Other is within.

We see the inverse of this logic at work in Michael Frayn's 1999 novel, *Headlong*, in which the protagonist desperately wants to believe that a painting he has come across is a lost masterpiece by Bruegel. When his research leads to ever-mounting anomalies between his painting and Bruegel's known works, rather than becoming discouraged by these inconsistencies, he reads them as support for his belief that he must indeed have a genuine Bruegel. How could it *not* be a Bruegel, he reasons, when it goes to such lengths to distinguish itself from a Bruegel?

In this case, it is difference that confirms its authentic identity.

Bozovic unites these opposing logics through Lacan's account of the dual nature of the subject's relationship to the signifier. The signifier, in one sense, Lacan contends, "petrifies" the subject by reducing its "being" into "meaning."[18] As Lacan explains, "when the subject appears somewhere as meaning, he is manifested elsewhere as 'fading,' as disappearance."[19] Yet at the same time, the subject is nonetheless the subject of the signifier, in the sense of being fully subjected to it through our utter dependence on the symbolic system—the "big Other." Because this system exists prior to our arrival, it always remains in some sense alien to us. As Sean Homer describes, "this Other can never be fully assimilated to the subject; it is a radical otherness which, nevertheless, forms the core of our unconscious."[20] The *Seinfeld* and Frayn examples highlight the signifier's inverse methods of commuting difference and equivalence. First, through the *Seinfeld* example, we encounter the signifier creating difference out of what appears to sameness. Rather than possess an intrinsic identity, the subject relies upon the precarious signifier—an entity whose relationships are held together by nothing more than mere convention—to provide the illusion of identity. Lacan demonstrates this function of the signifier through his well-known story of a brother and a sister, sitting face to face on a train next to the window. The train comes to stop, leaving the children to look out at the platform upon which stands a set of bathrooms, side by side. As Lacan tells it: "'Look,' says the brother, 'we're at Ladies!'; 'Idiot!' replies his sister, 'Can't you see we're at Gentlemen.'"[21] Only through the differences between their respective signifiers, the words "ladies" and "gentlemen," do the two apparently identical lavatory doors take on distinct meanings. Like subjects, the doors are not inherently differentiated; it is only the signifier that provides the illusion of difference.

In *Bodyworlds*, we primarily encounter the signifier in its function as making differences through the palpable recognition in the visitor that these organic bodies at which we look are not the same as the ones from which we see. Jacques-Alain Miller sheds additional light on this phenomenon through his discussion of the split that occurs during the mirror stage: "it's as if this visual totality, staggered by the relationship to the being there ... of its organism, was not a vital image but an already anticipated cadaver."[22] He continues by crediting the signifier with "allow[ing] the human animal to imagine himself as mortal ... to anticipate his death."[23] But the signifier not only enables us to see ourselves as mortal beings, it also provides a symbolic framework for keeping the horror of that immanence at bay. These two complementary functions of the signifier illuminate a key difference between Lacan's psychoanalytic account and Maurice Merleau-Ponty's phenomenological perspective regarding discussions of the mirror stage. As Vivian Sobchack puts it, Lacan emphasizes the "being seen" (the "object-me" reflected in the glass) over the "seeing being" (the "subject-I," standing in front of the glass), which is only constituted retroactively. For Merleau-Ponty, although the mirror stage primes us for seeing ourselves as objects, it nevertheless privileges the "seeing I" over the "object-me." Subjectivity, in this account, is buoyed up by an encounter with the object-self, by highlighting that what is required for us to recognize the object-me is a corporeal, "bodily presence before it."[24] In the case of *Bodyworlds*, this gap between subject and object is reinforced by the plastinates' sterility: although they are indeed human cadavers, they lack any visceral markers of corporeality.

The signifier's logic may strike us as more disturbing, however, when carrying out its inverse function: creating sameness out of difference. We see this second mode of the signifier in operation in Frayn's *Headlong*, where the painting was identified as a Bruegel through its very attempts at distinguishing itself from Bruegel's usual style. The ability to create sameness out of difference marks the uncanny logic of the signifier which operates in *Cloaca*. As Saussure emphasizes, there is no intrinsic identity between words and concepts; it is only the differential relationship among signs that enables the correspondence between words and concepts to emerge—that performs the function of making them appear the same. By contrast with *Bodyworlds*' sanitized corpses, which lack any visceral emanation, the mechanical *Cloaca* exhibits the mess and smell associated with the corporeal. In this sense, it is so much more like the untidy bodies that we occupy than the sterile plastinates that we encounter. It facilitates an encounter with the self as object through a nonmimetic, and specifically functional, realism. Support for this view can be found in the reaction of visitors to *Cloaca*, who, according to Delvoye, applaud "when the machine shits," an event that is not purely ocular but an olfactory experience as well.[25] Freud notes in *Civilization and Its Discontents* that although we are disgusted by the smell of another's shit, we are not bothered by the smell of our own. Perhaps, thus, we identify more intimately with this machine than we do with our fellow human beings. *Cloaca*, it seems, facilitates a disturbingly uncanny encounter with the same when we expect nothing more than an amusing novelty of difference.

But this encounter with "sameness," I argue, operates beyond the register of mimesis and occurs at the more disruptive level of mimicry. Drawing upon Homi Bhabha's distinction, mimesis functions as a form of representation "in the order of the model/copy," whereas mimicry is a repetition "in the realm of the simulacrum."[26] The plastinates in *Bodyworlds*, as we have argued, can be seen as mimetic copies of their spectators—albeit mimetic copies that ultimately assert spectators' distinction from them. This claim reinforces a view of verisimilitude in which a copy may be judged according to its fidelity to an original. But, if we draw upon Bhabha's insights, we encounter a view of mimicry that differs from a mimetic representational form that reproduces an original without altering it. Rather than merely instigating a question regarding the relationship between two distinct entities (as *Bodyworlds* does via mimesis), mimicry serves the more disruptive function of revealing the "non-coincidence of the same with itself."[27] Whereas the mimetic copy preserves, rather than threatens, self-identity, the simulacral product of mimicry disrupts the stability of the model itself. Through repetition, mimicry performs a simulacral operation of calling into question the identity of an original with itself. In this sense, while *Bodyworlds* preserves "the vital" difference between subject and object, *Cloaca* challenges the illusion of subjective unity by introducing the recognition of the "minimal difference" a subject has to itself—an awareness of the "split" that exists "at the core of the same."[28] The signifier gives rise to the "minimal difference" a thing or subject has to itself through its inability to perfectly match an element in the signifying system with the place it occupies.

The notion of "minimal difference" brings together the two functions of the signifier discussed earlier: George's excessive similarity to himself and the "lost" Bruegel painting's confirmation of sameness through difference. Both of these operations disturb the sense of coherence *within* a given entity rather than *between* one entity and another. I will argue that the minimal difference that appears as "the gap that separates a thing from itself, the gap of repetition" can be thought of in terms of the Lacanian Real.[29] As a process of the Real, Lacan adamantly distinguishes repetition (which operates at the level of the drive) from the Symbolic process of return/reproduction (which operates at the level of the symptom): "in Freud's texts repetition is not reproduction. There is never any ambiguity on this point: *Wiederholen* is not *Reproduzieren*."[30] Whereas return/reproduction occurs within conventional reality, in the order of automata, repetition appears as a Tuché from the Real—in Harari's words, as "an irruption [that] ... tear[s] th[e] blanket that reality constitutes for us."[31] Return occurs when a repressed element reappears via the signifier in a disguised form. For Roberto Harari, a key characteristic of return is homogeneity: although the symptom appears in a new form, no new element is introduced. Repetition, by contrast, performs a heterogeneous procedure in which difference is produced through pursuit of the same. Like return, repetition also involves an element of disguise, but here disguise enters in at the level of temporality rather than through content or form. In popular renditions of Freud, the psychic process of repetition appears as an effect of trauma: a traumatic event occurs and because it cannot be reproduced by (returned within) the signifying system, we are fated to repeat it. Lacan, by contrast, emphasizes that, rather than a result of trauma, repetition functions as a condition for trauma to emerge. The repressed trauma is installed retrospectively through the act of repetition itself. "What is repeated," Lacan emphasizes, "is always something that occurs ... *as if by* chance."[32] The repetition that inaugurates repression is rarely of the traumatic episode itself, but rather of an accident or coincidence of a seemingly insignificant magnitude—as Harari suggests, a match between the numbers on one's train ticket with one's birthday, for example. As Harari describes, "as innocent as it seems, the repetition of the same ending digit in the ticket numbers precipitates a traumatic situation because it may be construed as something inassimilable."[33] What initially appears insignificant at the level of importance becomes insignificant in the more disruptive sense of being unable to be made significant—unintergratable within the symbolic system. These events mark a missed encounter with the Real—a tuché—in which the unease of the Real "bursts in" to our reality and changes its perceptible coordinates. In Žižek's words, "although nothing changes, [as a result of this repetition] the thing all of a sudden seem[s] totally different. . . . If the Real is a minimal difference, then repetition (that establishes this difference) is primordial."[34]

The same thing suddenly appears uncannily different in the aftermath of repetition. In their most radical form, such encounters refract back onto the subject, delivering a destabilizing blow to the subject's illusion of individuation and coherence.

As a repetition in the psychoanalytic sense—a sameness with variation—mimicry produces an entity that is "almost the same but not quite."[35] But *Cloaca*, I suggest, pushes mimicry into the more "profoundly disturbing" order of "menace."[36] Mimicry shades over into menace when the balance between difference and sameness tips in favor of difference: the "almost the same but not quite" comes to appear as "a difference that is almost total but not quite."[37]

Why is the confrontation with "a difference that is almost total but not quite" more disturbing than an encounter with the "almost the same but not quite"? Bhabha's response to this question hinges on the relationship of disavowal to narcissism and paranoia: the "almost the same," his theory implies, is well accommodated by the process of disavowal. Disavowal enables subjects to manage well in the face of a disturbing encounter by providing the subject with the ability to hold together a contradiction—that is, I know very well that this looks like me, but even so I know that it is not me. On the other hand, Bhabha argues that the "difference that is almost total" gives rise to an "uncontrollable repetition of narcissism and paranoia."[38] For Bhabha, the subject in the grip of narcissism and paranoia engages in projection, rather than self-protection. The narcissistic/paranoid formation shakes up our reliance on the symbolic system and its ability to confer social position by installing the possibility of (narcissistic) identification with a figure of power and then introducing a (paranoid) sense of the arbitrariness of authority.

An encounter with the "almost the same" provides an opportunity to exercise the self-affirming procedure of abjecting—the process of expunging the other from the self. This operation works to uphold the illusion that subjective coherence is indeed attainable—once one rids oneself of unwelcome intrusions of otherness. The abject paradoxically becomes the necessary symptom around which the subject's illusion of cohesion is formed.

It enables the subject to inhabit the belief that, rather than a constitutive gap, the obstacle to unity can be expelled.

"Almost total difference," by contrast, confronts the subject with a more disruptive—"menacing"—encounter. The confrontation with an "almost total difference" raises the possibility that disunity might be a fundamental property of the subject. The idea that the subject may not be totally different than an object that appears to be radically different suggests that the subject may be, at some level, alien to itself. This phenomenon goes beyond pointing to the existence of something excessive within the subject, by moving toward the more disturbing possibility that there exists something intimate outside of the subject—an external dimension of subjectivity. As Harari elucidates, the Lacanian formulation of the unconscious as the discourse of the Other is a doubly externalizing phenomenon. Not only is the nub of subjectivity—the truth of the subject—located beyond the subject, it is also only ever encountered via the analyst in the role of *object a*[39]. Thus, rather than a subjectively recuperable experience of the discovery of an alien object in "I" (as we saw in the case of the "almost the same"), here we are faced with a radically desubjectifying phenomenon, in which the "I" is in the object. As Lacan describes, it is "at the anal level" that the subject "has the first opportunity of recognizing himself in an object."[40] Akin to the destabilizing encounter with the gaze as the impossible, external, place from which the subject sees itself seeing, *Cloaca* provokes an encounter with the subject as radically externalized in the object.

IF IT LOOKS LIKE A DUCK AND DIGESTS LIKE A DUCK …

Although it may be more comforting to locate our unique "humanness" in the ways in which we engage in more expansive activity than animals, Žižek observes that our humanness resides rather in the narrowest of our pursuits, namely, the drive. "We become humans," he argues, "when we get caught into a self-propelling loop of repeating the same gesture and finding satisfaction in it."[41] As a mechanical "organ without a body," *Cloaca* pursues a meaningless repetition, evoking what Lacan calls the "headless" drive and, as such, echoes the disturbing phenomenon of "subjectification without a subject," which characterizes the drive.[42]

A discussion of an early precursor to *Cloaca* sheds additional light on ways of thinking about the relationship between the human and the machine that simulates human processes. Jacques Vaucanson's *Digesting Duck* (1738) (or as Jessica Riskin terms it, "Defecating Duck") gained public notoriety in its day by pushing the genre of the automata from "amusement" to "philosophical experiment."[43] The Duck, as purported by its inventor, "'stretches out its Neck to take Corn out of your Hand; it swallows it, digests it, and discharges it digested by the usual Passage.'"[44] Vaucanson's piece was regarded as an attempt to go beyond "verisimilitude" by aiming for "simulation," "and thereby test[ing] the limits of resemblance between synthetic and natural life."[45] The sense in which Riskin refers to the Duck as a "philosophical experiment" resides in its ability to "simultaneous[ly] enact ... both the sameness and the incomparability of life and machinery. ... The defecating Duck ... dramatized two contradictory claims at once: that living creatures were essentially machines and that living creatures were the antithesis of machines."[46] According to Riskin, by appearing to embody functions unique to living creatures, the Duck did not succeed in blurring the distinction between the living and the machine, but rather worked to sharpen it. Historically, she argues, simulating automata have, no doubt against intention, succeeded in bringing to stark relief "precisely those capacities of living beings that ... [are] the likeliest to defy mechanistic reduction."[47] They have functioned, in a sense, to "sort ... the animate from the inanimate, the organic from the mechanical."[48]

Cloaca, however, fails to draw such palpable distinctions. In rejecting that his machine be read as a philosophical experiment and arguing instead that it be seen purely as an artistic amusement, Delvoye initiates a more disruptive encounter between the living being and the machine. Here, again, we confront the power of the double deception in facilitating a disturbance within the given symbolic order. The Duck, in turns out, merely dissimulated the processes of digestion and excretion. After much speculation, it was eventually revealed that the Duck did not actually process the food it "ate," but that a compartment of the machine was "loaded before each act with 'fake excrement'" to provide the illusion that digestion had occurred. By hyping a machine whose success turned on a simple deception, Vaucanson left both categories of the human and the machine firmly intact.

Delvoye, by contrast, did indeed produce a machine that simulates the organic process of digestion. But rather than tout his invention as an authentic representation of an organic process (as Vaucanson deceivingly did), Delvoye positioned his machine within the rhetoric and the appearance of fiction. In addition to *Cloaca*'s antimimetic appearance—it looks nothing like an organic body, but does what only an organic body does—Delvoye explicitly frames it within the symbolic context notoriously associated with deception: advertising. He uses the hyperbolic rhetoric of consumer culture to place *Cloaca*'s multiple iterations among other more familiar, much-hyped products: "Cloaca Original, Cloaca—New &

Improved, Cloaca Turbo, Cloaca Quattro, Cloaca No. 5, Super Cloaca and Personal Cloaca."[49] Cloaca also sports a variety of high-profile logos, citing, among others, Chanel No. 5, Coca-Cola, Mr. Clean, Chiquita Banana, and Harley Davidson, and in good marketing fashion, also spawns a range of spin-off merchandise: t-shirts, action figures, 3D view-master, toilet paper (and much, much, more!).

But perhaps the most compelling merchandise to follow (quite literally) from Delvoye's invention are the vacuum-sealed transparent bags containing *Cloaca*'s dried excrement, adorned with Delvoye's autograph, that sell for over $1,000 a turd. In this contemporary iteration of Piero Manzoni's infamous *Merda d'Artista* (1961), the artist's shit is replaced by the machine's shit.

By packaging the shit in clear plastic, rather than in a sealed aluminum can, Delvoye enacts a crucial variation on Manzoni's project. Manzoni's *Merda d'Artista* (priced at the going rate of an equal measure of gold) has long been thought to be a fake—a can devoid of the promised content. This suspicion gained momentum after the recent statement of one of Manoni's collaborators that the tins are filled with plaster rather than feces.[50] But, neither the veracity nor falsity of the product has yet to be documented due to the market logic governing the value of contemporary art.[51] The aluminum makes X-raying the cans impossible. This leaves opening the can as the only possibility for verifying the product, but this act would nullify the value of the object. In this sense, the contents of the cans are rendered effectually indeterminate. By packaging *Cloaca*'s turds in transparent bags, Delvoye makes a subtle nod at the "lingering uncertainty" surrounding Manzoni's work.[52] But through this playful association with the double-bind of Manzoni's work, Delvoye cunningly clouds his own formal claim to disclosure with a specter of uncertainty. Specifically, Delvoye plays upon the dilemma of authentication facing Manzoni's cans of professed shit by inverting it: *Cloaca*'s shit is offered in a transparent container, but this access does nothing to help adjudicate the ontological problem of its realism—is feces produced by a machine real?

Delvoye's *Cloaca*, thus, performs the disruptive logic of telling the truth in the guise of a lie.[53] On first consideration one might predict that, by casting in fictional allusion the machine's ability to repeat a uniquely organic process, Delvoye provided viewers with the opportunity for a comfortable, entertaining interaction with *Cloaca*. But, as we have encountered often in this book, fiction provides the optimal conditions for an encounter with the Real. Fiction provides the necessary lure for coaxing out the truth that evades symbolic capture. Lacan's formulation, "the non-duped err," points to the importance of recognizing that our sense of reality and subjectivity are sustained by a necessarily fictional support. We cannot arrive at the truth through abandoning fiction; we must enter into the fiction itself in order to cipher its logic in which the truth is embedded.[54]

The logic of the fiction presented by Delvoye entails a clever twist: he does not explicitly claim that the piece is a fiction, nor does he straightforwardly assert that it is real. Rather, he articulates the machine with other fictional productions/products, casting it with a sheen of doubt by association. Such an equivocation is deepened by the fact that any claims to veracity that may be made on *Cloaca*'s behalf attest not to its realism, but rather to its status as a proper simulation. Unlike Vaucanson's *Duck*, in which a fiction was presented as truth, Delvoye's *Cloaca* presents us with the inverse case of a truth presented within the context of fiction. Such a move points to how fiction provides the means to truth. Through its appearance as mere novelty, *Cloaca* succeeds in staging an encounter of "self-recognition" with "an object that bears neither [the subject's] image nor the marks of his individuation."[55] It succeeds in evincing the "objective core'" that lies at heart of subjectivity.

CHAPTER 7

"Something I Can't Quite Articulate"

Breastfeeding and the Real

Hanna Rosin's contribution to the April 2009 issue of *The Atlantic* entitled "The Case Against Breast-Feeding" created national outrage by questioning the medical literature on infant feeding upon which the mantra "breast is best" is based. Rosin herself is a mother who has breast-fed two children for longer than the minimum period that the American Association of Pediatrics recommends (and who, at the time of writing *The Atlantic* piece, was still breastfeeding her third child). She indicts what she sees as the guilt-inducing, scare-provoking rhetoric of modern breastfeeding discourse. In particular, she critiques the way that breastfeeding, even more so than eco-friendly commodities such as wooden toys and organic snacks, has become the "real ticket to the club" of committed, urban, middle-class motherhood. She reiterates with particular acuity familiar arguments regarding the labor implications of the classist contemporary rhetoric surrounding breastfeeding when she contends that breastfeeding is "a serious time commitment that pretty much guarantees that you will not work in any meaningful way. [The time you spend nursing] adds up to more than half of a working day, everyday, for at least six months. . . . [W]hen people say breastfeeding is 'free,' I want to hit them with a two-by-four. It's only free if a woman's time is worth nothing."[1] Rosin's article really pushes buttons, however, not through the vigor of her political economic critique, but through her wistful conclusion. Her attempt to make sense of why she has persisted with breastfeeding in the light of what she comes to see as hyperbolic interpretations of its benefits and its immense attendant difficulties ends on a poignant note: "My guess," she suggests, "is something I can't quite articulate. Breastfeeding does not belong in the realm of facts and hard numbers; it is much too intimate and elemental . . . even part-time, it's a strain. But I also know that this is probably my last chance to feel warm baby skin up against mine, and one day I will miss it."[2]

This chapter circulates around the tension between Rosin's confessed failure to adequately articulate an explanation for why she continues to breastfeed and her compelling arguments against breastfeeding, which detail how class privilege stealthily haunts both the discourse and the pragmatics of breastfeeding. The key intervention will be to use Rosin's struggle to explain her attachment to breastfeeding as a way to understand why breastfeeding is a culturally and psychically fraught practice. In particular, I argue that a Lacanian psychoanalytic approach to analyzing the rhetoric surrounding breastfeeding can bring to light underappreciated dimensions that supplement a political economic analysis.

Through a Lacanian psychoanalytic lens, I will argue that the inability to put into language why one breastfeeds should not be seen as a failure on Rosin's part to find the appropriate words; breastfeeding is an act that stretches the logic of the Symbolic without ascending into the realm of the Romantic ineffable. It thus evokes anxiety in participants and spectators alike, a specifically Lacanian variety of anxiety, not born out of a sense of lack, but rather an anxiety that strikes when the lack *required* for the subject's emergence appears itself to be lacking. In breastfeeding, the necessarily lost object (a role which the breast comes to play) is encountered.

In what follows, I suggest that mainstream breastfeeding advocacy efforts in the United States miss this crucial aspect of breastfeeding and thus are unable to address the question of why it is such a psychically fraught practice. To make this case, I will explore the rhetoric of breastfeeding advocacy in two contexts: (1) the US government's 2004 National Breastfeeding Awareness Campaign; and (2) La Leche League International. Although both of these programs have contributed significantly to encouraging breastfeeding, I argue that because they fail to account for the ways in which breastfeeding stages an encounter with the lost object, each, in a different way, fails to confront a key obstacle to the widespread acceptance of breastfeeding. In particular, I will argue that the US government campaign deploys a politics based upon the logic of factual representation ("facts and hard numbers"), the realm that Lacan designates the Symbolic order. The approach used by La Leche, by contrast, constitutes a politics based upon the logic of what Lacan calls the Imaginary realm, which appeals to the fantasy of total unity and specular identification. I will suggest that, instead of a politics grounded in the Symbolic or the Imaginary, breastfeeding promotion requires a politics derived from the logic of what Lacan calls the Real (an approach to which Rosin's piece unexpectedly points us). For Lacan, the Real designates the dimension that lies beyond signification, the zone of shades left behind by the repression of the lost object (paradigmatically the breast).

In these discourses surrounding contemporary American breastfeeding practices, we encounter manifestations of what Rancière calls "the representative regime." This regime governs relationships of visibility and perceptibility that limit possibilities for what is "sayable" as well as the allowable correlations between actions and images. Breastfeeding, we will see, is framed primarily in terms of either scientific discourse (as employed by the government advocacy campaign, which carries the logic of the Symbolic) or of attempts to appeal to romantic/sentimental connections between mother and child (as proffered by La Leche League by calling upon the realm of the Imaginary). When these discourses strike impasses—in particular, when they are unable to account sufficiently for the socioeconomic dimensions of modern breastfeeding (as I will show)—an additional move might be called for: namely a shift from the representative regime to what Rancière calls "the aesthetic regime." Such a shift unsettles the constraints governing the representative regime's hierarchical organization of who is accounted for and who is rendered invisible, as well as which actions are seen as possible in relation to particular images and statements. My contention will be that although Rosin's *Atlantic* essay has been widely regarded as apolitical at best and reactionary at worst, it might be properly considered as a missive that performs exactly this political work by disrupting the limited framework of the conventional representative regimes and offering new possibilities for engaging with breastfeeding as a contradictory and psychically/socioeconomically fraught practice that is tinged by the Real.

This chapter thus extends questions raised by previous work on the limitations of breastfeeding advocacy—limitations not only at the level of its efficacy and inclusiveness, which Rebecca Kukla discusses, but also limitations that, as Elisabeth Badinter argues, it places upon women's autonomy. In particular, I contribute a psychoanalytic perspective to illuminate breastfeeding not solely in terms of its cultural, political, and economic components but also as a practice with profound psychic dimensions. This approach allows me to extend the analysis beyond the usual question of why women *do not* breastfeed even when it has become a social imperative to do so, to examining the question of why women *do* breastfeed even when that imperative is not persuasive.

Here again we encounter an example of how the lie paves the way to the Real. In this case, the unconvincing and often unfeasible arguments made by breastfeeding advocates provide a glimpse of the truth of desire and anxiety that may attend Western breastfeeding practices. The continuing practices of breastfeeding in the light of the failures of both the Symbolic and the Imaginary to provide a "realistic" framework within which it is normalized help locate it as an act resonant with the Real. Through this approach, I aim to uncover not only additional concerns within existing advocacy rhetoric but also to provide new insights into how breastfeeding may resonate with women in ways that have not been explored previously.

The cases I examine here are limited to the two main strands of breastfeeding advocacy in the United States. This does not constitute a major restriction on my analysis, however. As Badinter notes, in Europe advocacy discourse is not greatly different, although there is generally greater compliance with national breastfeeding recommendations than in the United States (a variation frequently attributed to family-friendly governmental policies).[3] In particular, in her polemic against the constraints modern notions of motherhood place upon women, Badinter argues that breastfeeding advocacy campaigns across Europe and North America share an emphasis on breastfeeding as the key marker of a "good mother" and that in both the European and North American contexts, appeals to both ecological and economical interests are invoked as supplementary justifications.[4]

THE NATIONAL BREASTFEEDING AWARENESS CAMPAIGN AND THE LIMITATION OF THE SYMBOLIC

The National Breastfeeding Awareness Campaign can be read psychoanalytically as one among several possible strategies to palliate the anxiety associated with a confrontation with the breast as the paradigmatic lost object (which Lacan situates in the domain of the Real). One of the most effective ways to protect against the anxiety that emerges from the overproximity of the lost object is to encapsulate it within a symbolic scaffold.[5] By building a case for breastfeeding based on rational appeals to facts and figures, the US government breastfeeding campaign attempts to do exactly this: inscribe breastfeeding within the lists of the Symbolic. Joan Copjec, in her account of the "aura of anxiety that surrounds" eighteenth-century breastfeeding advocacy, argues exactly along these lines; in particular, she asserts that the incorporation of breastfeeding into "Oedipalized space ... infuse[s] it with an air of interdiction, of rules, regulations, and prescriptions and yet it offers us relief from the constricted, asphyxiating space [of] *zusammenschnueren*."[6] Copjec points here to the ways in which the law of the Symbolic can interrupt the suffocating presence of the proximate object.

But the enduring cultural unease surrounding breastfeeding indicates that these efforts to claim breastfeeding for the Symbolic have not been fully successful. As Kukla confirms, breastfeeding rates within the United States "fall well below the targets" identified in the government campaign, as well as being "well below the rates in all other developed countries."[7] Consumer culture in the United States provides telling examples of this lack of success. The specific anxiety surrounding exposure of one's breasts during public breastfeeding has spawned a whole industry of concealment products. Perhaps the most well known of these products is the "hooter hider," an "award-winning nursing cover, [which] was born out of necessity when . . . [its creator] found nursing her infant daughter in public challenging."[8] But the products fail to allay anxiety. Indeed, their continuing commercial success is evidence for and thus depends upon exactly this failure.

A more recent product, the "booby beanie," has recently garnered considerable media attention. The "booby beanie," a knitted baby hat that looks like a giant breast with a protruding nipple-shaped top, seems to openly mock the imperative to conceal the breast. When worn on the head of a nursing baby, the "booby beanie" caricatures the breast upon which the baby sucks. In Slavoj Žižek's sense, then, we may think of the "booby beanie" as contributing to the ideologically subversive act of "overconformity."[9] By conspicuously announcing and exaggerating the object that it dutifully conceals, the "booby beanie" performs an overly literal attachment to the "law." The "booby beanie," thus, calls the bluff of the proscription to keep the nursing breast concealed by following the injunction to the letter, while violating its spirit. Such acts of overconformity, Žižek argues, work to undermine the law by making explicit its premises that only function if they remain implicit.[10]

Copjec offers an explanation for this failure: symbolic incorporation, she tells us, is necessary but not sufficient to keep at bay the anxiety triggered by an encounter with the lost object (and with the Real, more generally). An additional move is required:

> In order for the symbolic to evict the real . . . it is necessary to say that the real is absented, to declare its impossibility. . . . The symbolic, in other words, must include the negation of what it is not . . . [which] means . . . that the symbolic will not be filled only with itself, since it will also contain this surplus element of negation.[11]

Copjec contends that the only way that the Symbolic can perform the necessary act of "negation" is through repetition, in particular, through the "signifier's repeated attempt—and failure—to designate itself."[12] She then goes on to suggest that a key way in which the Symbolic works to include the rejection of impossible elements is accomplished by prohibiting that which is already impossible.

An example of this approach can be found in Žižek's observations regarding the paradoxical structure of the cultural rhetoric surrounding child sexuality. Here, he claims, we encounter the "prohibition of something which is already in itself impossible. . . . [Childhood sexuality, we are told] does not exist, children are innocent beings, that is why we must control them strictly and fight child sexuality."[13] The prohibition, thus, inscribes "its 'repressed' point of reference" through its excessive and senseless repetition of the impossible.[14]

In the case of the government advocacy campaign, we see that the impossible is not so much prohibited through its repetition, but rather required. That is, in acknowledging and defending against breastfeeding's many challenges, the government campaign *mandates* rather than prohibits the impossible. In particular, the National Breastfeeding Awareness Campaign does this by drawing upon romanticized notions of the mother–child bond (derived from the Imaginary zone of fantasy) in order to supplement the appeal to rationality. In particular, it emphasizes the importance of breastfeeding as a way of experiencing "joyful bonding with your baby" and "perfect nutrition only you can provide." [15] The Campaign's website announces, for example, that "many people feel warmth, love, and relaxation just from sitting next to a mother and baby during breastfeeding."[16]

The campaign, thus, frames the sentimentalized (or what Lacan calls "The Imaginary") in terms of the pragmatic (Symbolic), by pointing toward the practical challenges of breastfeeding: physiological complications, the need to return to work, and the lack of community support. But the campaign also replies to these practical challenges by listing pragmatic advantages such as "cost savings" and "health benefits for both mother and baby."[17] By thus acknowledging breastfeeding to be a logistically and culturally complex practice, affected profoundly by dynamics of class and privilege, and by providing encouragement and useful (hard-to-come-by) information about ways to navigate its various difficulties, the campaign goes some way toward easing the anxiety associated with breastfeeding. But, I now argue, both of the contrasting strategies that the government program deploys for framing breastfeeding—the sentimentalized (Imaginary) and the pragmatic (Symbolic)—fail to account for its psychic dimensions, and thus fail to disperse the anxiety surrounding it. This, I will argue, is evident in both the impossibility of the constraints that the campaign implicitly imposes upon breastfeeding as well as the residual discomfort that accompanies it both by the mother and the public.

The campaign makes gestures to encourage women to feel comfortable when breastfeeding in public. We are reminded that "it isn't possible to stay home all the time and you can feel free to feed your baby while out and about. You should be proud of your commitment! Plus, no bottles and formula means fewer supplies to pack!"[18] Here the campaign quite rightly indicates that a policy of exclusive domesticity would be impossible. But in its place they implicitly install another impossible requirement: one's breasts must never be exposed during the act. In the light of the unpredictability and frequency of babies' feeding needs, a mother and baby would have to stay home all the time in order to be certain of avoiding breastfeeding in public. As Bernice L. Hausman, author of *Mother's Milk: Breastfeeding Controversies in American Culture*, pointedly remarks, "to have breastfeeding promoted by medicine and the government with the social stipulation that one must not appear to be doing what one is doing is a tall order indeed."[19] The importance of discretion in public breastfeeding is illustrated by the campaign's website, which provides a list of suggestions for feeding without exposing the breast.

Their suggestions include the following: using a "special breastfeeding blanket around your shoulders"; "breastfeed[ing] your baby in a sling . . . it makes it easier to keep your baby comforted and close to you"; "slip[ping] into a women's lounge or dressing room to breastfeed"; and "practice[ing] at home so that you can ensure you are only being as revealing as you feel comfortable with [sic]."[20]

It is worth noting that these are presented as suggestions only for allaying the potential discomfort of the nursing mother. Awkwardness about exposure is rarely located on the side of the public (they, after all, should be gleaning cozy vibes from being in the presence of the feeding dyad!). Hausman takes up this question of the public's hidden stakes in discrete forms of breastfeeding. She recounts that often when people express the importance for discretion while breastfeeding, their

> comment is . . . followed up by a description of a woman who was not discreet in her public nursing, which is generally perceived to be an embarrassment for the nursing woman, rather than for the storyteller, who is clearly the one experiencing the embarrassment. But why insist that one is embarrassed for another?[21]

Here Hausman suggests that this displacement of embarrassment from the public to the mother is a "blaming gesture." I suggest that it is more than that. In addition to functioning as an act of blame or as a disingenuous remark deployed to conceal one's own discomfort, embarrassment for another performs a fundamental psychic and cultural function.

It acts simultaneously as a marker of one's disturbing encounter with the Real of the lost object and a defense for withstanding that disturbance. Embarrassment, specifically one's *announcement* of feeling embarrassment at what amounts to an other's proximity to the Real, serves to protect one's own sense of being at a safe distance. In particular, I suggest that the frequency of remarks of the sort to which Hausman draws our attention indicates that breastfeeding confronts spectators—even ones who are in favor of it—with an unsymbolizable dimension from which they seek cover.

In this context it is noteworthy that although unease regarding the possibility of exposure during public breastfeeding is one of the most frequently cited reasons women give for why they stop or never start breastfeeding, the campaign website does not make a more significant contribution to allaying this fear by emphasizing women's legal protection. In particular, rather than underscoring a woman's legal authorization, the campaign touts empowerment based solely on one's personal choice and conviction.[22] To be specific, using individualist rhetoric, the government campaign acts as a cheerleader, encouraging mothers to embrace their personal decision to breastfeed. For example, when it comes to the category of addressing difficulties surrounding breastfeeding in public, mothers are told that "it is important to believe in yourself and your choice. Remind yourself that you can succeed and wear your confidence!"[23] Such individualist rhetoric warrants ideological, and specifically, feminist critique. But more than that, it serves as an example of how the campaign shies away from achieving its own stated goals. In particular, although the narrative section of the government website encourages a woman to feel comfortable breastfeeding in public, it fails to detail the extent of the legislation that protects a mother's right to do so.

Thus, it appears at first that the government campaign merely mandates the minimally permissible, encouraging the most conservative notion of what is already culturally acceptable. Yet, on closer inspection, their emphasis on tips for discreet feeding, coupled with the omission of detailing codified, legal protections, implicitly reinforces the taboo of the exposed breast. And because the erratic and squirmy movements of hungry babies mean that even women with a deep commitment to discretion (swathed in protective "hooter hiders") will expose their breasts, it seems again that breastfeeding becomes the site of an impossible requirement.

Another anomaly accompanies public reactions to exposure during breastfeeding. The amount of bodily exposure that occurs in most instances of breastfeeding is significantly less than the accepted revelation of the female breast in mainstream media and culture. Such disproportionate reactions might suggest that rather than the exposed breast itself, what is dreaded is the exposure of the female breast in a desexualized, nurturing context. This proposition sheds light on the following puzzle: why do dress codes allow the female breast to be largely exposed as long as the nipple is concealed? Nipples, rather than their surrounding mounding flesh, are shared by both men and women. Thus, if the goal is to eliminate a sexualized view of the breast, one might expect that codes of decency would require that the skin surrounding the nipple be concealed, rather than the nipple itself. That this expectation fails to be met suggests that the sight of a woman's nipple is unsettling, not so much because of any sexual connotations, but rather because of its functional role as an orifice for milk.

The rhetoric of the government initiative surrounding public breastfeeding is permeated with such anomalies that, in psychoanalytic terms, amount to a logic of disavowal: "I know that x, but even so not x." Disavowal enables one to cope with a reality that is too threatening to fully incorporate into our consciousness. One always and already "knows" the thing that one disavows (or else there would be no need to disavow it), but because one cannot comfortably inhabit that knowledge, one disavows it. Disavowal enables us to live with knowledge that would otherwise be too threatening to bear. We see exactly such a structure of disavowal in the case of breastfeeding: "we know very well" that of course it is acceptable if the breast becomes exposed during breastfeeding (how could it never not?), "but even so," one should avoid this from ever happening (because it would make both the mother and onlookers uncomfortable); "We know very well" that breastfeeding is a vital and loving act of nurturance, "but even so," I do not want to see what is really taking place. The prevalence of such disavowals signals that, in breastfeeding, we are at risk of an encounter with the Real—an occurrence that imperils the illusion of symbolic closure.

In short, none of the suggestions made by the government campaign achieve what Copjec requires for enabling subjects to cope with brushes with the Real: namely, the prohibition of the impossible. Instead, the campaign offers a series of ultimately unsatisfactory defenses against a Real that always and already returns in the displaced form of new challenges and sources of anxiety.

LA LECHE LEAGUE INTERNATIONAL AND THE IMPOSSIBLE RETURN TO THE IMAGINARY

Founded in 1956 as an alternative resource to the dominant "medical model" of breastfeeding, La Leche League International (LLLI) remains the leading organization for promoting and supporting breastfeeding worldwide through advice imparted "from mother to mother." As they describe, "Our Mission is to help mothers worldwide to breastfeed through mother-to-mother support, encouragement, information, and education, and to promote a better understanding of breastfeeding as an important element in the healthy development of the baby and mother."[24] Although they occasionally offer tips for feeding "discretely," the tenor of their rhetoric is distinct in their commitment to advocating "complete breastfeeding," a view of breastfeeding as a "relational process."[25] For La Leche, not only is the mother's milk essential for the baby, but the mother's continual physical presence is also vital. They advocate the mother's "minimal separation from the baby, few supplemental bottles (if any), and feeding on the baby's demand."[26] Their commitment to privileging the physical connection between mother and child has led the League to frown upon any sort of "substitutes for the bodily comfort" that the mother can provide, including not only apparatuses associated with the baby's oral needs such as "bottles and pacifiers" but also the use of equipment such as "playpens and carriages."[27]

Like the US government's National Breastfeeding Initiative, La Leche mandates, rather than prohibits, the impossible. But, instead of operating through an appeal to the Symbolic (the realm governed by the logic of factual signification), La Leche promotes breastfeeding in terms of its connection to the Imaginary realm (governed by the fantasy of unity and specular identification). And similar to the government campaign, the requirement for what "counts" as "true" breastfeeding within the La Leche's framework is virtually unachievable,[28] particularly within the US context, where at best, women are given only twelve weeks of unpaid leave under the Family and Medical Leave Act.[29] As a result, La Leche has come to dispense advice on pumping milk for babies to consume when the mother is not present, but this practice is nearly always framed as one that should be used only in cases where it is absolutely necessary for a mother to return to work. In other words, financial necessity rather than professional fulfillment is taken as the relevant reason for a mother of a baby to work. Along these lines, La Leche encourages families to explore ways of cutting household expenses by providing money-saving tips in order to spare women the need to return to work. As Hausman describes, "because the practice of breastfeeding promoted by the League is so all-consuming, the authors have a difficult time incorporating a positive assessment of working-mothers within its purview."[30]

La Leche risks excluding women who are unable to weather the financial implications of forgoing paid work outside the home or who work for reasons that transcend instrumental economic rationale. But their acknowledgment that exclusive breastfeeding is often incompatible with working outside of the home does draw attention to the economic privilege required for sustaining exclusive and attached breastfeeding. Such recognition of the economic toll of breastfeeding backs up Rosin's violent attack upon the dominant discourse that perpetuates the myth that breastfeeding is free: "[w]hen people say breast-feeding is 'free,' I want to hit them with a two-by-four. It's only free if a woman's time is worth nothing."[31]

KellyMom, a prominent and frequently cited Internet resource for information on breastfeeding, features a page that serves as a representative example of this dominant breastfeeding advocacy rhetoric. Under the heading "Financial Costs of Not Breastfeeding ... or Cost Benefits of Breastfeeding," KellyMom enumerates the money saved by not buying formula, both in raw figures and in terms of commodities that can be purchased for the "equivalent buying power" of "the cheapest formula costs."[32] For example, by the end of day two of her baby's life, an exclusively breastfeeding mother has saved enough money to buy a "video rental, book, or magazine"; by two months the savings amount to "new clothes for mom, microwave oven, or baby play yard"; by seven months she has saved enough to accrue a "new dining room set"; and by nine months of exclusive breastfeeding, she has saved the equivalent of a "washer/dryer or 3 night Bahamas cruise for mom, dad & baby."[33]

In her cost-benefit analysis, the writer of KellyMom limits the costs of breastfeeding to a tally of "optional" aids one can purchase, such as nursing bras, dresses, pillow, stool, and breast pump. Commodities appear here as the only "costs" of breastfeeding; the labor cost (as Rosin laments) remains invisible. In short, it seems clear that the argument for exclusive breastfeeding as a "cost-effective" practice (apparently aimed at a woman for whom such savings would matter) works paradoxically to naturalize the class privilege necessary for a woman to opt out of paid labor.

Although La Leche's insistence on the importance of the mother's physical engagement with the child provides a refreshing antidote to the "disembodied" rhetoric of the government campaign, and the dominant discourse with which it is aligned, it falls into similar traps. Linda M. Blum, in her path-breaking book, *At the Breast: Ideologies of Breastfeeding and Motherhood in the Contemporary United States*, laments the turn to "disembodied motherhood" that attends dominant discourses promoting breastfeeding in the twentieth-century United States. In Blum's view, the government campaign, with its emphasis on providing working women with opportunities and physical spaces to pump milk (rather than on extending the duration of paid work leave or the construction of on-premise child care facilities), "fetishizes" mother's milk. "Through this fetish," Blum argues, "the mother is disembodied, as if she *is* the milk; by providing this milk, she still qualifies as an exclusive mother, *as if* mother and baby are monogamous and physically tied."[34]

I will suggest that more than fetishizing mother's milk, La Leche winds up creating a fetish out of maternal embodiment itself. In Freudian terms, a fetish operates through the mechanism of disavowal, described earlier, that enables a subject to cope with a difficult reality. To be specific, a fetish enables a subject to simultaneously hold together a conscious knowledge (in Octavio Mannoni's formula, "I know") and the belief that it is not really so ("nevertheless . . . ").[35] A fetish thus operates as a liminal zone between illusion and reality; it provides a subject with a comforting (but illusory) substitute for an unbearable/impossible reality. How, then, can maternal embodiment itself take on the role of fetish? By emphasizing the need for the continuous presence and unity with the mother's body, *even outside of the feeding relationship*, I suggest that La Leche's mandates surrounding maternal embodiment enable us to locate a key anxiety precipitated by the act of breastfeeding. In particular, in its advocacy of the continual bodily copresence of mother and child beyond the context of feeding, La Leche can be seen as (unintentionally) attempting the impossible: reduplicating the intertwining of bodily boundaries that necessarily occurs in utero, the loss of which (according to Freud) constitutes the originary (repressed) trauma.

In other words, La Leche's call for the virtually uninterrupted continuation of the mother–child dyad works to deny the bodily separation of the birth event, and in so doing, appeals (more or less covertly) to the fantasy of primordial unity, associated with the Lacanian realm of the Imaginary. Unlike the Symbolic, which attempts to mediate the Real by installing distance between the subject and the overproximate object, the strategy of the Imaginary involves creating the illusion of unification with the always and already lost object. In a sense, the Imaginary works to create a retrospective illusion that the object once had a definite presence and wholeness, and then offers a form of return to this originary state. Whereas the government campaign's appeal to science, medicine, and legal rights attempts to inscribe breastfeeding within the safety of the Symbolic realm, La Leche tries to mitigate the anxiety of breastfeeding by an appeal to this Imaginary unity.

In particular, La Leche performs a disavowal of the discomforting reality that the two discrete bodies of mother and child are nonetheless physically dependent upon one another: we know, of course, that the mother and child are no longer physically tied, but we nonetheless act as if they were.[36] The Imaginary reduplication of the fetal relationship that is enabled by this disavowal helps to mask the excessive element of breastfeeding. In short, La Leche downplays the rhetoric of "empowerment by choice" that the government campaign pushes and instead situates the postbirth feeding relationship exclusively within the framework of the Imaginary—as continuous with the fetal feeding relationship. Such a maneuver helps make breastfeeding appear as both necessary and inevitable, rather than a symbolically infused, rationally calculated choice.

The continued bodily connection between mother and child, even outside of breastfeeding, that is involved in La Leche's vision of "embodied motherhood" works to disembody the mother by denying her the full range of bodily movements, connections, and enjoyments that are incompatible with bodily attachment to the child. The League provides a compensatory rhetoric for this loss by "gently endors[ing] breast-feeding pleasures" and "sensuality."[37] Blum recounts a passage from the most recent edition of La Leche's book, *The Womanly Art of Breast-feeding* (2004), in which the sensual side of breastfeeding is addressed more explicitly:

> Breast-feeding is intended to be a pleasurable experience for a mother. A woman who breastfeeds with pride and satisfaction is aware that breast-feeding is a sensual experience. She also knows that this is a perfectly healthy and normal aspect of her sexuality.[38]

Here by privileging the depth and range of the mother's physical connection to the child, maternal embodiment is presented as what amounts to a fetish that enables the transformation of the unbearable Real (the impossible *return* to the presymbolic unity of the mother–child dyad) into a bearable reality (the *continuing* bodily bond).

In sum, I am arguing that breastfeeding threatens to confront us with an unbearable excess: namely, the bond of nurturance that, occurring invisibly in utero, appears excessive when it is no longer biologically required. The insistence on maintaining other forms of uninterrupted contact between the baby and mother helps to lessen one's sense of this excess. Why? Because when a mother is able to come and go, when she can pursue desires beyond the child, the Imaginary illusion of mother–child total unity is irredeemably disrupted. In this context, La Leche's requirement of "complete breastfeeding" may be read as a mandate for the impossible *return* to mother–child unity. By seeking to create *continuity* with the mother–child dyad, their program works to undermine the uncanniness of encountering this impossible return.

BREASTFEEDING AND THE REAL

In the light of these arguments, we can now return to Copjec's argument that Oedipalizing an anxiety-laden act works to assuage anxiety in the specific context of breastfeeding. In particular, I question whether, in the case of breastfeeding, the introduction of the Symbolic, as in the government campaign, might precipitate rather than palliate anxiety. Copjec's suggestion for allaying the anxiety of the Real via its "domestication" in the Symbolic seems predicated on the usual assumption that the Symbolic realm operates to smooth over the fissures created by the Real. But La Leche's appeal to the Imaginary realm in calling for continuous postbirth physical binding of the mother and child prompts us to consider a complication in this standard position. The analysis of La Leche's rhetoric points to the prospect that in the case of breastfeeding, the arrival of the Symbolic itself is what must be diminished in order to keep anxiety at bay. Such a proposal requires us to reevaluate Copjec's thesis. Specifically, it raises the possibility that breastfeeding presents us with a fundamental exception to the usual appeal to the Symbolic as an aid in coping with the threat of the Real.

It is tempting to respond to this point by looking to the Imaginary as a means of allaying the anxiety of breastfeeding. And indeed, the Imaginary register presents us with a different path for an "impossible attempt to escape the various manifestations of the Real that threatens disintegration of one kind or another: trauma, loss, anxiety and so on" than the one offered by the Symbolic.[39] Unlike the Symbolic, which attempts to mediate the Real by installing distance between the subject and the overproximate object, the strategy of the Imaginary involves creating the illusion of unification with the always and already lost object. In a sense, the Imaginary works to create a retrospective illusion that the object once had a definite presence and wholeness, and then offers a form of return to an originary state of unity with it. Whereas the government initiative's appeal to science, medicine, and legal rights attempts to inscribe breastfeeding within the safety of the Symbolic realm, La Leche, I have argued, tries to mitigate the anxiety of breastfeeding by exactly such an appeal to the Imaginary. That is, rather than try to distance us from the overproximity of the lost object, La Leche's rhetoric invokes the fantasy of a return to pre-Symbolic Imaginary unity with the lost object.

In sum, whereas the government campaign operates along the same lines as the eighteenth-century breastfeeding advocacy that Copjec analyzes, by "seek[ing] to submit the child not to the mother but—quite to the contrary—to the social law," La Leche's rhetoric attempts to submit the child solely to the mother by mitigating the unwelcome intrusion of "law."[40] Both of these approaches, I have argued, are unsuccessful in squelching the anxiety provoked by the surfacing of the Real. In what follows, I suggest that these two strategies—one deploying the resources of the Symbolic and the other drawing upon the mythos of Imaginary wholeness—face a unique challenge in the case of breastfeeding, a suggestion which also points to an exception to Copjec's thesis that Oedipalization (the introduction of the Symbolic) is a step toward assuaging the anxiety created by encountering the Real.

A Lacanian account of the role of the lost object, as what he calls the *objet petit a* (of which the breast figures as an example par excellence) sheds light on why breastfeeding provides us with an exceptional case for the inevitability of failure on the part of both the Symbolic and Imaginary to ease anxiety. The *objet petit a* operates as a property of the body from which we must separate ourselves in order to become subjects.[41] As an instantiation of the *objet petit a*, the breast functions as just such an "extimate" object—an object that is "simultaneously the intimate kernel and the foreign body; in a word, it is *unheimlich*."[42] But the temporal status and ontological consistency of the *object petit a* is trickier than this initial account reveals. The *object petit a* is not simply the object whose eventual renunciation marks the subject's emergence. It is an object that is *created by* the subject's entry to the Symbolic. It follows the logic of the future anterior in that it "will [retroactively] become what it was. . . . The Lacanian answer to the question, from where does the repressed return, is then paradoxically: from the future."[43] To put this in concrete terms, it is only through the subject's emergence into the Symbolic that the breast, retrospectively, becomes an *object petit a*. Thus, the breast as object is not, in any romantic sense, ineffably beyond signification. Rather, as we will see, the complication it poses for signification arises because it is foundational to signification. It cannot be properly signified due to its function as the object whose retrospective loss becomes the *cause* of signification. Its loss propels the child to enter the Symbolic realm and accede into subjectivity. Likewise, the breast as *object petit a* is not the object of desire for the subject, but rather the object whose perceived lack *causes* the subject to desire—inaugurating the subject's (futile) quest for an object to satisfy her perceived lack.

As Roberto Harari emphasizes, this Lacanian notion of the breast as lost object differs from Melanie Klein's view of the breast as a fully present object whose eventual loss influences a subject's subsequent psychic life. The Kleinian position holds that the subject and object once coexisted, until the moment at which the object is no longer present, such as in the transition from breastfeeding to weaning. By contrast, for Lacan, the breast never existed as an object while it was present; it can only become an object—*object petit a*—at the moment at which it no longer exists for the subject. As a lost object, the breast emerges not as a marker of the subject's separation from the mother, but rather of division internal to the subject herself/himself.[44]

Marie-Hélène Brousse emphasizes that "when one speaks of an object, one is speaking of a lost object."[45] The breast, thus, must be appreciated for its role in marking a liminal dimension that is neither clearly the property of the mother nor of the child. In Harari's cogent description, it comes to function as an *object petit a* through "a corporeal automutilation from which the subject is separated, 'in a matter which is to a certain extent internal to the sphere of its own existence' with the aim of thus being able to constitute itself."[46] This insight highlights why the romantic notion of mother–child symbiosis, offered to us by appealing to the Imaginary, is of little comfort. An appeal to Platonic complementarity—to reuniting with one's "other half"—cannot heal the rift of internal division. The subject is not missing an "other," but rather a fragment of itself. This is why Lacan insists that "the most decisive moment in . . . anxiety, the anxiety of weaning, is not so much when the breast falls short of the subject's need, it's rather that the infant yields the breast to which he is appended as a portion of itself . . . during breast-feeding the breast is part of the individual who is being fed. . . . It is merely stuck onto the mother."[47]

In Lacanian terms, human beings must sacrifice the "immediacy of . . . *jouissance*, as well as access to that primordial object of completion which is the mother" in order to emerge as fully fledged subjects.[48] The Symbolic both precipitates and compensates for this loss. In the Imaginary the baby lacks nothing but must cope with its utter dependence on the mother by imagining that it is as "indispensable to the mother as she is to it."[49] Only when the child senses that the mother has needs of her own and experiences itself as having needs that are not met does the child accede to enter into the symbolic world, in hope of finding what it lost. As Bruce Fink puts it:

> if nourishment is never missing, if the desired warmth is never lacking, why would the child take the trouble to speak? As Lacan says . . . "what is most anxiety producing for the child is when . . . there is no possibility of lack, when its mother is constantly on its back." Without lack, the subject can never come into being.[50]

Lack, therefore, enters onto the scene as a *cause* of the subject's entry to the Symbolic, not solely as its *effect*. It is, then, the lack of this lack—felt when the "lost" object appears to have returned—that threatens to devastate the security of the objective world. The unbearable pleasure of jouissance turns out to be the price the subject pays for grounding in the objective world. In the face of this necessary but hefty sacrifice, the encounter with an entity (the breastfeeding mother–child dyad) that appears to have access to direct jouissance—that appears as the impossible "unbarred" subject—becomes unbearable.

I suggest that our customary rhetoric surrounding weaning implicitly divulges these Lacanian truths; in particular, it reveals the intolerability of an encounter with the impossibility of a subject who has entered the symbolic without having paid the requisite price of jouissance. It is customary to say glibly that breastfeeding should end "when the kid can ask for it." But why? Why is the acquisition of speech an appropriate indicator of the need to wean, any more so than a variety of other developmental milestones? Why is the image of a talking, breastfeeding subject so unsettling? My guess is that this conventional wisdom guards us from encountering the impossible Real that accompanies breastfeeding: the appearance of a fully fledged subject who has not sacrificed immediate jouissance.

POLITICS

I conclude by considering what sort of political approach might be most effective for breastfeeding advocacy. The government approach is dominated by a politics of the Symbolic, which attempts to distance us from the Real by embedding breastfeeding within the rational world of facts and figures. La Leche League International draws heavily upon the logic of the Imaginary, which aims to domesticate the Real through an appeal to the mythos of primordial incorporation. What is absent from both of these discourses surrounding breastfeeding is what Glyn Daly calls a "politics of the Real." Such an approach does not aim to negate or incorporate the impossible object, but rather endeavors to engage with the ways that the persistent existence of this disruptive dimension is fundamental to our sense of reality. It involves inhabiting the recognition that the Symbolic order is itself founded on impossibility and that any appeal to its totality is an illusion. The appearance of Symbolic wholeness is produced only through the exclusion of objects that challenge its consistency. In particular, the Real must be excluded for reality to exist. A politics of the Real must face this exclusion, and specifically it must acknowledge that the Other (the Symbolic world) is necessarily lacking. Thus, by contrast with frequent characterizations of the Real as a terrifying thing that *causes* the symbolic system to stumble, Lacan emphasizes that the Real is the *effect* of the constitutive failure of the Symbolic to flawlessly render reality.

Although largely read as a manifesto against breastfeeding, perhaps Rosin's *Atlantic* article contributes to such a project of breastfeeding advocacy from the side of the Real. Rosin both demonstrates the shakiness of the scientific literature upon which breastfeeding advocacy draws and dismantles the romantic appeal to mother–child symbiosis through a devastating political-economic critique. What she is left with is the "irrational" truth that none of this has compromised her own desire to continue to breastfeed.

Here, I suggest, Rosin's unexpected conclusion embodies the Lacanian notion that "truth" exists at the point where knowledge fails. Paul Verhaeghe powerfully captures this Lacanian distinction between knowledge (which exists in the realm of the Symbolic) and truth (which is a property of the Real):

> [there is a] difference between knowledge and something beyond knowledge, something that belongs to another register, other than the symbolic order. . . . there is something that cannot be put into words, something for which words are lacking. . . . the essential characteristic of truth is that it confronts us with the ultimate point where knowledge about desire . . . can no longer be put into words. . . . This dimension beyond the signifier is the Lacanian real.[51]

Against expectation, therefore, Rosin's piece might turn out to provide one of the most compelling public accounts of how breastfeeding can be appreciated for its engagement with the Real. Through the pursuit of a desire that she cannot "quite articulate," Rosin engages with the irrational passions that exceed the romantic image of mother–child symbiosis and are antithetical to her "knowledge" of the exaggerations of breastfeeding's benefits. We see here how "truth" emerges not from knowledge, but rather from its failure—its points of deception. Rosin's "The Case Against Breastfeeding" disrupts the symbolic closure that it seeks to perform and, in so doing, touches profoundly on the Real that propels one to act according to one's desire. This is not the ineffable Real that romanticized readings of Lacan foreground, but rather a Real that, in its disruptive effects upon the Symbolic order, opens up a space in which new ways of ordering the world can be entertained. This is not a positively articulated alternative, perhaps, but rather a leap into a new domain of thinking, away from established ideological patterns.

As I suggested earlier, Rosin's provocation may also be seen in terms of Rancière's aesthetic realm. Her piece creates a dissensus by unsettling the dominant frameworks within which breastfeeding is located, the scientific (Symbolic) and the sentimental (Imaginary), and presses upon the points of exclusion within these frameworks. Her intervention, thus, lies not simply in voicing the socioeconomic contradictions that are ordinarily suppressed or inadequately accommodated but also in challenging the tenability of the discourses through which such exclusions are secured. Thus, rather than attack these dominant perceptual systems from outside of them, she troubles their logic from within, thereby, in Rancière's terms, disrupting the expected relationships between what is sayable and what is possible.

CHAPTER 8

Melancholia and the Real of the Illusion

Lars von Trier proclaims that his 2012 film, *Melancholia*, concludes with the "happiest ending he's ever made"[1] and Slavoj Žižek declares *Melancholia* a "profoundly optimistic" film.[2] In the light of these remarks, it might surprise those unfamiliar with the film to learn that *Melancholia* centers on a morosely depressed woman, Justine (Kirsten Dunst), who, on the brink of the apocalypse, abandons her husband and her job at her wedding. The film concludes with the destruction of the Earth via a cosmic collision with the stealth planet, Melancholia. How, then, are we to make sense of von Trier's and Žižek's comments? In this chapter, I suggest that their comments can be understood in terms of the way the film provides fresh possibilities for living ethically in the face of loss and the collapse of the big Other, possibilities best appreciated in terms of what Lacan elaborates as the "feminine" position of sexuation.

These political possibilities may not be readily apparent due to the spectacularly distracting nature of the film's content. *Melancholia*, as has been frequently remarked, is characterized by stunning extremes in an affective register but also at the level of narrative construction and form. Yet, on closer inspection, the hyperbolic spectacles presented in the film provide a key to understanding the interpretation of the film offered by von Trier himself and by Žižek. To be specific, I argue that the film's excesses point us toward a reading of it as a triumph of the "feminine" logic in offering an ethical response to loss, which deploys the strategy of masquerade as a response to the impossibility of symbolic totality. This reading focuses upon the hyperbolic fiction of the film, not in order to see through it to reveal an underlying reality, but rather in order to highlight the "nothing" that it titivatingly purports to conceal.

Viewing the film within the framework of the feminine logic of sexuation also offers a way of making sense of von Trier's assertion that *Melancholia* is a "women's film." This contention has often been read as a reference to the film's deployment of the conventions of "melodrama" and the "gender patterns" exhibited by its characters.[3] I will argue that *Melancholia* is a "women's film" in another sense: it offers a lesson in the triumphant logic of the Lacanian sexuated position of woman over that of man. As I indicated earlier, the positions of woman and man, for Lacan, have nothing to do with biological or even cultural identities, but they should be understood as psychic orientations to lack, specifically as ways of accommodating the failure of the Symbolic order as a totalizing system capable of grounding our identities. In particular, Lacan tells us that the Symbolic always fails in one of two ways: either it is incomplete or it is inconsistent. And, he adds, that "every speaking being situates itself on one side or the other" of this failure: subjects psychically aligned with the "masculine" pole of sexuation respond with a strategy of imposture to the inconsistency of the Symbolic order, and those aligned with the "feminine" pole of sexuation respond to the Symbolic order's incompleteness with a strategy of masquerade.[4]

Steven Shaviro touches upon Lacan's schema of sexuation as a lens through which to view the film when he comments on how the two key "'alpha-male' characters are both unmasked as impotent impostors."[5] As I indicated, in Lacan's account, man's approach is characterized by imposture—an authoritative display of empty but resonant signifiers of power, so as to hide the fact that there is "nothing" securing one's symbolic identity. The two "alpha-man" characters referred to by Shaviro are Justine's sister, Claire's (Charlotte Gainsbourg) husband, John (Keifer Sutherland), and Justine's boss, Jack (Stellen Skarsgård). John, the exorbitantly wealthy owner of the vast mansion and estate where the wedding is held (and also where they live), has supreme confidence in the scientific prediction that Melancholia will not strike Earth and zealously awaits the once-in-a-lifetime, spectacular sight of seeing it "flying by" Earth. His confidence is as ostentatious as his wealth, but when he discovers that the scientists, whose authority he has been drawing upon for his own credibility, are wrong and that Melancholia will indeed crash into Earth, he cannot face the failure. He abandons his family and kills himself in the horse stables.[6]

The bombastic Jack is similarly exposed as a weak fraud. He offers Justine a promotion at her wedding, but she bluntly rejects him and demeans his authority, calling him "a despicable, power-hungry little man." He is left speechless and manages to respond only by petulantly smashing a plate to the ground.[7] In short, the film reveals imposture to be a precarious strategy for covering lack: it involves fastidious effort to maintain the illusion of a robust big Other that can fully guarantee symbolic completeness but is easily imperiled. Because it leaves no room for error, even a minor challenge can lead to its absolute and unbearable collapse.[8]

To explore the seemingly surprising claims that von Trier and Žižek make in connection with *Melancholia*, I begin by considering the film's violation of generic expectations. It has been frequently remarked that, although *Melancholia* is a film about the end of the world, it nevertheless departs from the typical Hollywood "disaster film." Chris Peterson, for example, argues that the film positions itself as "an antidisaster disaster film."[9] Hollywood disaster films, Peterson points out, tend to invite the spectator to "participate in the fantasy of living through one's own death," whereas *Melancholia* "leaves us with no survivors, thus depriving the spectator of the routine pleasures afforded by the disaster genre."[10] Here Peterson is referring to the way in which the film concludes with a black screen at the exact moment of the catastrophic collision of Melancholia into Earth.

Such a bleak ending seems to trouble Žižek's and von Trier's reading of the film as "happy" or "optimistic." But, on second glance, despite the grim ending, the film opens a space for optimism. Although we are faced without any surviving character with whom to identify, we, as audience, live on. As Peterson points out, "due to the mechanical reproducibility ... this performative annihilation bears a capacity to repeat itself before innumerable spectators."[11]

Thus, the filmic medium's ability to infinitely reproduce the end of the world seems to put viewers at a considerable advantage. Although we are left "bereft of any living protagonist with whom we can identify, we nevertheless survive."[12] André Bazin, I indicated earlier, confronts this dimension of mechanical reproducibility in the context of death in "Death Every Afternoon," in which he reminds us that "on the screen the toreador dies everyday."[13] Through the filmic medium, even the most singular of events becomes a daily regularity—part of what Lacan calls "the automaton."

In *Melancholia* the recurrence of the singular event of the end of the world is not reserved for repeat viewings but is included within the film itself. The apocalyptic conclusion to *Melancholia* appears first within the diegetically unintegrated prologue. The film begins with a visually stunning, slow-motion, lyrical prologue, set heavy-handedly to the overture of Wagner's *Tristan and Isolde* in which the film's denouement is revealed in magnificent fashion. The prologue serves neither as a background nor as a supplement to the film, however, but rather offers an alternative mode of telling the same story. As Neil Maizels puts it, "there is almost a sense in which these opening moments make the rest of the film redundant."[14] When the final scene of the film occurs, we already know (even if the characters do not) that the planets will collide because this has been revealed to us in the opening sequence. The climactic ending thus functions as a return to what has been anticipated rather than as a conclusion.

Trauma, as Bruce Fink describes, follows the logic of the future anterior: it emerges as something that "at a certain future moment . . . will have already taken place."[15] Trauma, in this sense, is retrospectively constituted through the act of its return "from the future," as Žižek describes it.[16] Similarly, for the spectator of *Melancholia*, the prologue offers an engagement with something that "will have happened," which, I suggest, rather than preparing us for the conclusion, makes it more disturbing, indeed constitutes it as a trauma. In Žižek's terms, we may say of the interplanetary collision that "before it actually happened, there was already a place opened, reserved for it in fantasy-space."[17] To be specific, before the fatal, final moment has appeared on screen, the space of the event was already prepared for us by the dreamily expressive prologue.

A second way of justifying Žižek's and von Trier's claims regarding the film's "optimism" is to consider it as an allegory of the intolerable experience of deep depression. Indeed, Von Trier suggests exactly this when he claims that *Melancholia* "'is not so much a film about the end of the world; it's a film about a state of mind.'"[18] In discussing *Melancholia*, Peterson refers to the conventional view that an allegorical reading is "comforting" because it makes the destruction of humanity seem "unreal." From this point of view, the film goes beyond the simple avoidance of trauma to serving a "prophylactic function" against trauma.[19] We may elaborate this idea of the film as a deterrent against trauma by recalling Freud's suggestion that anxiety can function as a "sort of inoculation" against real trauma.[20] In particular, drawing upon Freud's account of anxiety, we may say that, as an allegory, safely removed from the real thing, the film incites precautionary anxiety in the spectator, so as to avoid a disturbing encounter. In Freud's terms, the film "vividly imagines the danger situation . . . with the unmistakable purpose of restricting that distressing experience."[21]

The film itself explicitly comments on the possibility that anxiety serves to protect us from a real threat. Claire, the anxious sister, envies the melancholic Justine for her preparedness for the catastrophe. In particular, as she frets about the likelihood of the apocalyptic disaster to her unruffled sister, Claire bitterly expresses her jealousy, chiding Justine: "Oh, you have it easy, don't you?" Here the film seems to suggest that melancholia provides a stronger shield against catastrophe than anxiety. We will return to this question shortly in the context of exploring how the film represents the two psychic structures of anxiety and melancholia as responses to immanent disaster.

Many critics have argued that the apocalyptic theme as an allegory for the profound, immobilizing depression is too heavy-handed to be effective. As Peterson points out, the film as a "metaphor for . . . severe depression . . . is about as subtle as being hit over the head with a two-by-four'" (a metaphor that itself is about as subtle as being hit with a two-by-four). Similarly, in his scathing critique of *Melancholia* as "the only real dud among the films [shown at Cannes in 2011]" Colin MacCabe denounces the film as a "pastiche [that] uses every cliché in the book" (as if "in the book" is not a cliché) whose characters "seem like caricatures," and whose theme of "damning the bourgeoisie [is] so hackneyed that you wonder how von Trier persuades great actors to so demean themselves."[22] But, I contend, rather than undermine the film's power, it is through the overt exaggerations and the commitment to hyperbole that we encounter the film's ethicopolitical potential.

To make this argument, I reverse the usual direction in which the allegorical argument is made: rather than read the apocalyptic as an extended metaphor for morbid depression, I turn this around to consider how Justine's melancholia and Claire's anxiety can be seen as allegories for the end of the world. Each sister demonstrates a psychic formation that offers opportunities for assessing how a subject may cope (or not) with radical loss.

I begin with the tactics that the melancholic has at her disposal for managing trauma. Von Trier, insisting as he often does, that the role of the most miserable woman in his film is indeed autobiographic, tells us that the inspiration for the character of Justine emerged from his own analysis. He was struck by the therapeutic insight that "melancholics will usually be more level-headed than ordinary people in a disastrous situation, partly because they can say: 'what did I tell you?'"[23] Through her behavior, the melancholic Justine indicates that she has been preparing for the apocalyptic interplanetary disaster long before anyone could have known about it. She is depicted as having withdrawn interest from objects, goals, and relationships that are meant to make life meaningful, long in advance of their absence. This, as Claire resentfully points out, makes it easier for Justine to accept their actual loss. The only thing that we see bringing comfort—and perhaps even jouissance—to Justine is the approaching of the eponymous planet, Melancholia. As it nears, she basks blissfully naked in its glow, her depressive inhibitions beginning to fade. By contrast, when Justine is deep in the throes of her unbearable depression, she is unable to muster the energy to lift her foot high enough to enter into a bath that she would have previously enjoyed, and she can no longer eat her favorite food (meatloaf), declaring that it tastes of ash. But, once Justine becomes certain that Melancholia's path will intersect catastrophically with Earth, her appetite returns: we see her unreservedly enjoying jam by repeatedly sticking her finger directly into the jar and then right into her mouth.

Prior to her spirits lifting in the wake of Melancholia's imminence, how was Justine's psychic melancholia serving her? Slavoj Žižek contends that "against Freud, one should assert the conceptual and ethical primacy of melancholia."[24] In opposition to the mourner, who integrates loss into the Symbolic realm, the melancholic remains faithful to the "remainder" that cannot be integrated. As Lacan puts it, in melancholia, the mourning process "doesn't come to a conclusion because the object takes the helm . . . [the object] triumphs."[25] But, Žižek points out, the melancholic confuses "loss" and "lack," in that the object that appears lost is really not an object at all, let alone one that the subject possessed. What the subject misses is the constitutive lack that no object had ever fulfilled. Because the object that appears to have been lost was not only never possessed but also has never existed, the mode of honoring it takes the form of deception. For Žižek, this melancholic deceit occurs in both form and degree: melancholics treat "an object that we still fully possess as if this object is already lost" and the magnitude of their mourning can be characterized as "a faked spectacle of the excessive."[26]

Now we can turn from the melancholic Justine to the anxiety-ridden Claire. What protection is afforded to Claire by virtue of her anxiety? The comparison between anxiety and mourning emerges pressingly at the end of Freud's paper *Inhibitions, Symptoms, and Anxiety*.

As Lacan puts it, at the end of this seminal paper, "Freud wonders in what way everything he has put forward on the relationship between anxiety and object loss is distinct from mourning," and he goes on to devote the "entire addenda . . . to *Inhibitions, Symptoms, and Anxiety* [to this] most extreme awkwardness."[27] In particular, Freud powerfully asks, "When does separation from an object produce anxiety, when does it produce mourning, and when does it produce, it may be, only pain?"[28] Freud follows up this inquiry immediately with the comment: "Let me say at once that there is no prospect in sight of answering these questions."[29]

I will argue that these questions, especially regarding the relationship between melancholia and anxiety are illuminated by the relation between Claire and Justine. Both melancholia and anxiety involve a complex relation between deception and temporality, which straddle both retrospective and anticipatory trajectories. In melancholia, as we discussed, the subject institutes a loss as a way to engage with and attempt to manage lack. The melancholic withdraws interest and affect from the objects she still has, in anticipation of her loss. As I indicated, Justine dramatically threw away all the things that seemed meaningful in her life: her job, her marriage (at her wedding), and the good will of her friends and family.

In anxiety, we encounter an inversion to this structure: rather than introduce a loss in order to manage a retrospective lack in the fashion of the melancholic, the anxious subject institutes a lack in order to prepare for an impending loss. Thus, by contrast with the melancholic who mistakes constitutive lack for mere loss, the anxious subject treats impending loss as a threat to her lack. The deception is deepened by anxiety's inoculating function: it is in a sense by pretending that the danger has already struck, that one can avoid it really hitting. Anxiety, in Freud's words, involves both "an expectation of a trauma . . . and a repetition of it in mitigated form."[30]

Here, again, we are faced with a form of deception, which we can understand via an engagement with Lacan's account of anxiety. Lacan takes Freud's explanation in the direction of highlighting the way in which lack itself functions as the foundation of subjectivity. Consequently, Lacan qualifies the Freudian description of anxiety as a "reaction to the danger of a loss of an object,"[31] telling us, rather, that "anxiety isn't about the loss of the object but its presence"; it strikes when a positive object appears where lack should be.[32] As Lacan repeats frequently throughout his *Anxiety* seminar, rather than being associated with the loss of an object, "anxiety is not without an object." By "object" here, Lacan means the *objet petit a*, which plays the vital role of regulating and palliating the subject's relationship to the Real. To this he adds, anxiety strikes whenever this object fails to sustain the subject in a tolerable relationship to lack. The object can no longer tame the threat of the Real if it fills the place of lack too fully.

Lacan, thus, reformulates anxiety as the "lack of lack." He emphasizes that "anxiety isn't the signal of lack but of something that has to be conceived of . . . as the failing of the support that lack provides."[33] The danger to which anxiety points, then, is that of losing the lack. For example, Lacan explains, the most distressing thing for an infant is not the mother's absence, but of her over-presence. What provokes anxiety is "everything that announces to us . . . that we're going to be taken back onto the lap . . . the most anguishing thing for the infant is [if] the relationship upon which he's established himself, of the lack that turns him into desire, is disrupted . . . when there's no possibility of any lack, when the mother is on his back all the while."[34]

As such, for Lacan, anxiety shares a close relationship to doubt: although anxiety is itself "free of doubt," it nevertheless is "the cause of doubt."[35]

This deep connection with doubt stems from the certainty that anxiety brings. As Lacan puts it, anxiety is "that which does not deceive";[36] it is "the only thing to target the truth of . . . lack."[37] One way to understand this Lacanian relationship between doubt and certainty is to appreciate that when faced with the real of anxiety, the subject looks for some way out. But, as Lacan attests, "as regards anxiety . . . there is no safety net . . . each piece of the mesh . . . only carries any meaning insofar as it leaves empty the space where anxiety lies."[38] The subject, in the throes of anxiety, clings to doubt as an attempt to "snatch from anxiety its certainty."[39] But, as we will see, this doubt only entrenches us more deeply in certainty.

A pivotal scene from the film can be read as a chilling manifestation of Lacan's insight here, that in "the effort that doubt expends . . . to combat anxiety . . . what it strives to avoid is what holds firm in anxiety with dreadful certainty."[40] After being promised by John that Melancholia has safely passed Earth and should be receding, Claire's sense of doom remains unshaken. In an attempt to introduce doubt as a weapon to combat her terrifying certainty, she picks up a wire contraption made by her son, Leo, which he uses as a gauge to tracking Melancholia's distance from Earth. If John is to be believed, Melancholia will appear smaller when viewed through Leo's metal ring. But when Claire puts the ring to her eye, the rogue planet alarmingly fills the hole completely, signaling its increasing proximity to Earth. Thus, her attempt to introduce doubt winds up confirming the "dreadful certainty" of her anxiety. The image of the planet appearing fully in the hole where lack should be vividly illustrates Lacan's refrain that anxiety occurs when "something . . . appears . . . [in the place of the lack] because lack happens to be lacking."[41]

This encounter with the certainty of anxiety is untenable for Claire, and it sets her off on a frantic attempt to somehow escape the unavoidable catastrophe. Her acting out appears to take the form of a massive disavowal; when faced with knowledge that Earth will be destroyed, she nevertheless attempts to take Leo and leave the grounds of her vast property. This impossible attempt ends with Claire collapsing to the ground while struggling to bear Leo's weight in her arms, breaking down with grief at the futility of escaping the immanent horror—a scene depicted in heart-wrenching slow motion in the prologue.

This is not the only example within the film of Claire exhibiting disavowal. When Justine bluntly tells her that she knows the world is coming to an end, that "life is only on Earth and it's not for long," Claire responds, "but where would Leo grow up?" This moment is characterized by Peterson as a "disavowal . . . at once poignant and darkly comic. What part about the world coming to an end does she not understand?"[42] One could turn this around, however, and say that it is precisely Claire's ability to understand perfectly what is meant by the end of the world that prompts the need for her acts of disavowal. Thus, it seems, Claire is like the fetishist who is a realist because she has found a mechanism for enabling her to face the truth.[43] But, I argue, this approach is unsuccessful for Claire because, despite appearances, she is neurotic, not perverse. Lacan prepares us for this reading when he tells us that when faced with anxiety, it is not unusual for the neurotic to appropriate the perverse fantasy as an approach to "defending himself against anxiety . . . keeping a lid on it."[44] But, we learn, the perverse fantasy doesn't suit the neurotic—in Lacan's words, it "becomes him much like gaiters do a rabbit."[45] The perverse fantasy at issue involves having "things . . . in their right place. . . . the *a* . . . right where the subject can't see it and the capital S is in its place."[46] The neurotic, thus, puts himself in the place of the *objet a* but never succeeds in "mak[ing] much of [t]his fantasy" as a defense against anxiety.[47] Why not? Because the *objet a*, which helps neurotics manage their relationship to lack, also functions as "the bait with which they hold on to the Other."[48] Ultimately, the perverse fantasy fails for the neurotic because the "neurotic won't give up his anxiety."[49]

It is this unyielding grasp for the Other that rests at the heart of how we might cope with the loss of the Other. And here we return to a version of the question with which we began: namely, what the film might demonstrate regarding possibilities for coping with or refusing to cope with radical loss. This returns us, too, to ethical-political questions regarding "feminine" and "masculine" responses to symbolic impasses, which might lend support for von Trier's and Žižek's positive remarks regarding the film's ending.

Steven Shaviro offers a tempting interpretation of how the film concludes with a triumph of the feminine logic. When it becomes clear to all the characters that Melancholia will indeed collide with Earth, Leo becomes appropriately terrified and explains to his aunt, Justine, that his father had warned him that if the planet struck, "there would be 'nothing to do,' . . . 'nowhere to hide.'"[50] Justine eases Leo through the horror of the catastrophe by telling Leo that his father must have forgotten about the one place where they will be safe—the "magic cave," which Leo keeps asking "Aunt Steelbreaker" (as he refers to Justine throughout the film) to build with him. In their final moments, Justine, Leo, and Claire build the magic cave, a teepee-like structure of tree branches, under which they sit and hold hands until the deadly collision strikes.

Shaviro analyzes Justine's final act as a consummate feminine gesture. Justine, he argues, "offers Leo an exception—a kind of Lacanian 'feminine' supplement."[51] Many critics point to this as a "redemptive" moment in the film. Maizels, for example, writes that "Justine finds her modicum of salvation from melancholia in a brief maternal gesture to her sister's little boy, keeping some structure of meaning and hope alive within him, long after it has flown from his parents and herself."[52] In particular, Shaviro links Justine's ability to step outside her intractable depression in order to comfort the child as a "gesture to [the] 'fantasy of the future.'"[53] Here Shaviro invokes "what Lee Edelman calls reproductive futurism": a heteronormative structure of values in which the "figure of the child [is posited] as the promise and guarantee of 'social and cultural survival.'"[54] Edelman advocates for the ethical function of the queer as a threat to "the future" that the child secures.

Seductive and compelling though this reading may be, I object to Shaviro's interpretation on two grounds. First, this act does not follow the feminine logic developed by Lacan, or at least not for the reason he gives. Secondly, the ending of the film points not to the fantasy of reproductive futurism, but rather to a way to inhabit fully the ultimate destruction.

As a prelude to my first objection, I argue against the temptation to equate kindness with the ethical. What Justine does for Leo is an act of tremendous compassion, but that does not necessarily qualify it as an ethical act in the Lacanian sense. A Lacanian ethical act does not aim to reaffirm the fantasy of wholeness (as Justine's erection of the magic cave seems to do). Rather it serves to abandon the fantasy that such wholeness is attainable. In particular, contrary to Shaviro, Justine's testament to the existence of an exception that can preserve the symbolic order may be understood as a "masculine" act: the invocation of an exception, which serves to stitch the incompleteness of the symbolic together. Here, I agree with Zahi Zalloua's account of the "male logic" as characterized by "exception" and of the female logic as making "no claim of universality rooted in exception."[55] Thus, if we see Justine's suggestion to build the magic cave as a promise of an exception to the zone of destruction, then her actions fall within the masculine logic, in which the exception functions as the external guarantee required to knit together a whole. The feminine pole, by contrast, refuses the totalizing exception and instead inhabits the impossibility—the not-all, which characterizes the truth of the Real.

Against Shaviro, I will suggest that, although Justine does indeed (as he claims) act according to the feminine logic, it is definitely not on account of mobilizing an exception. On the contrary, my contention will be that her final act of constructing the magic cave follows the logic of the feminine by carrying out a masquerade, which attests that only illusion can guarantee the Other.

Before developing this argument in more detail, let us briefly return to the second objection I have to Shaviro's account, namely my disagreement that the ending functions as a comforting nod to "reproductive futurism." I will argue that a reading of the film as happy and optimistic is justified not because it points to a comforting possibility, but rather because of its stark facing of reality. The palpable fear exhibited by Leo, the proverbial "innocent child," at the moment he registers that the end of the world is near, drives home the inescapable reality that Claire disavows throughout the film: that with the end of the world comes the end of sexual reproduction. Justine, who seems to have not only already accepted this nothingness, but has luxuriously basked in its glow, is able to facilitate acceptance of this fate for Leo and (perhaps to a lesser extent) for Claire.

CONCLUSION

Each of the three characters, Claire, Justine, and Leo, comes to face the inevitable in his or her own way. As Peterson notes, "each character . . . embodies a different mode of comportment toward the absolute end . . . yet none of these modes are presented to us as necessarily more authentic . . . than the others."[56] Before Leo voices his fear to Justine, Claire makes a suggestion for how to enter into the nothingness: they should spend their last night together "on the terrace" with "a glass of wine"—an arrangement which, notably, excludes the child. This plan attempts to uphold the big Other at the very moment of its definitive destruction. The proposal is fitting for Claire; a neurotic in the throes of anxiety will attempt to conjure the big Other as a misguided attempt to both ward off loss and disguise its nonexistence. Justine responds harshly to Claire's plan, calling her idea "shit" and suitably retorting, "Why don't we meet on the fucking toilet?" Justine's crude rejoinder evinces a disregard for civilization—an institution secured via prohibitions issued on behalf of the Other—appropriate on the eve of the end of the world. Rather than cling desperately to the resources of the Symbolic, like Claire, Justine flouts the imminent meaningless of cultural conventions.

In carrying out an act that attempts neither to reinstall symbolic authority nor to reject its efficiency, Justine, I submit, undertakes a potentially transformative engagement, aimed at the very point at which the symbolic ruse gives way to the Real. In making this point, I reply to a question that Peterson raises of who, exactly, the magic cave is for: is it only for the child or does Justine also "require a symbolic bulwark against destruction"?[57] This question of who effectively "believes" in the power of the magic cave overlooks the way belief functions as a binding mechanism, without the need for any subject to identify as the one who believes. All that is required for belief to hold together the social-symbolic network is the belief in the existence of a subject who *really does believe*—a "subject supposed to believe." As Žižek describes, belief is "always minimally 'reflective,' a 'belief in the belief of the other. . . . In order for the belief to function, there *has to be* some ultimate guarantor of it, yet this guarantor is always deferred, displaced, never present *in persona*."[58]

The question of who it is who actually believes evades the crucial point that the mere illusion of belief suffices to secure its binding function. Justine's construction of the magic cave can be understood as a fundamental embrace of exactly this constitutive power of illusion. This, in turn, suggests a reading of the film's apocalyptic ending as an acceptance of the triumph of the Real over reality, which, rather than positing the Real as undermining reality, positions the Real as "an illusion which irrationally persists against the pressure of reality."[59] The conclusion of the film, thus, falls squarely in line with Lacan's notion (drawing upon Joan Riviere) of the feminine masquerade. In building the magic cave—an overt artifice (invoked by Leo throughout the film as a game)—Justine highlights that the efficacy of the big Other is sustained only through fiction. Critiques of the film for its inauthenticity are thus turned around: rather than simply posing a limitation to the "reality effect," we may read *Melancholia*'s exaggerations as a key to decoding the feminine logic of how to live within the horizon of the Real that undergirds the film, as well as pointing to an alternative interpretation of *Melancholia* as a "women's film." By simultaneously inhabiting and flaunting the artificiality of our most binding illusions, the film's ending demonstrates a way to live within the contradiction of the not-all, which characterizes woman's relationship to the Symbolic order.

In this sense, the film can be read as a parable for dealing with the loss of the Other, which protects us from the Real. If the film can, indeed, be seen as happy or optimistic, I suggest that it is in the sense that, in a hyperbolic way, it reveals the condition of all subjects; we are all always-already both marred and sustained by lack and living both in the aftermath and on the brink of loss. The beauty of the film, for Žižek, lies in its expression of the possibility that one can come to "accept . . . that at some day everything will finish, that at any point the end may be near."[60] Rather than degenerate into nihilism, Žižek suggests that the film shows that "this can be a deep experience which pushes you to strengthen ethical activity."[61] I concur that the "profoundly optimistic" quality of the film emerges from its demonstration of how a subject can live, and live ethically, in the light of this full recognition.

Conclusion

On Being Duped

The preceding chapters suggest a way of understanding Lacan's famous dictum that "the non-duped err." They offer a glimpse of the political possibilities afforded to those who, rather than seek to overcome the duplicity of the Symbolic order by "seeing through" its deceit, allow themselves to be taken in, to be duped by it. As subjects, we must contend with the fundamental deceit of the Symbolic order: our existence both depends upon the signifier and yet we are perpetually "barred" by it. How one copes with this bind of being both inside and bound to the socio-Symbolic order, and outside and not-fully accounted for by it, can take at least two forms.

The cynic, the subject who "sees through" the deceit, is duped by failing to recognize that his or her ability to see through to how things "really are" matters very little, indeed merely preserves the status quo. This is because the cynic overlooks the way in which reality is not structured by the way "things really are," but rather, by the symbolic fiction that props up reality. In endeavoring to see under the ideological mask, the cynic fails to recognize that it is the mask itself that organizes the social world.

By contrast, the duped, the subject who accepts the fiction of the Symbolic order, is "wise." Rather than seek to uncover a true reality behind the symbolic façade, the duped inhabit Žižek's insight that "the social mask matters more than the direct reality of the individual who wears it."[1] The dupe avoids the trap of believing that she can outsmart the efficiency of the symbolic ruse. In other words, the subject who allows herself to be duped, who avoids believing that one can step outside the illusion, inhabits the truth that, deceitful or not, it is the symbolic fiction that structures reality.

We can see the advantage of allowing oneself to be duped throughout the book. In each case, the attempt of the nonduped to see through deception leads to a misplaced trust in the possibility that one can encounter the truth by stepping outside the socio-Symbolic order. It is, by contrast, the move of the wise, the dupe, to find the ways in which the truth is structured by the very deception of the Symbolic order. By following through the path of the duped, one does not gain access to (the impossible) unmediated reality, but one can encounter the truth of how "reality itself has the structure of a fiction" in that it is symbolically constituted.[2] It is only by committing to this path that we can reach the Real that defies integration into the symbolic universe—that functions as the very impasse which shapes our engagement with "reality." It is only by grasping the forms that this symbolic failure takes that we can encounter the specter of the constitutive antagonism informing our reality.

Žižek compellingly explains this phenomenon as it occurs in Claude Levi-Strauss's example from *Structural Anthropology* in which native inhabitants of a South American village are asked to draw a map of their village. One group depicted the village as having houses arranged in a circle, and the other group drew two housing areas divided by a border. The "reality" of the layout of the village could easily be determined, Žižek points out, by viewing it from above in a helicopter. But hiring a helicopter to adjudicate the situation would be the mistake that the cynical nonduped subject would make. By endeavoring to look behind (or above) the fiction in order to "obtain the undistorted view of reality," the cynic misses the truth.[3] It is only the duped subject who, by entering into the fiction of how the village is laid out, can arrive at the truth—the Real of the distortions that shape how reality is perceived. As Žižek tells us, "This is what Lacan has in mind when he claims that *the very distortion and/or dissimulation is revealing*: what emerges via the distortions of the accurate representation of reality is the real, i.e., the trauma around which social reality is structured."[4]

The "symbolic fiction," which mediates our access to reality, provides a framework for smoothing over the fissures and antagonisms that threaten to destroy reality's coherence. But rather than try to step outside of the symbolic fiction in order to look at reality objectively, it is only by submitting to the authority of the fiction that we can chance upon the constitutive gap—the truth of the Real shapes our perception of reality. But further insulation of the Symbolic to the intrusion of the Real is provided by an additional component of the symbolic fiction: it perpetuates the idea that it *is* possible to occupy an "objective," "meta" position from which reality can be properly adjudicated. By being lured by this option, the nonduped is unwittingly lead down a path of deception. This trap prevents him from finding the truth, which lies not outside, but *within* the fiction.

Roland Barthes was known to have "valorized Lacan's dictum that 'the non-duped err'" and his late lecture series, *Comme Vivre Ensembles (How to Live Together)*, addresses this phenomenon in the resonant context of Palladius's 419-20 story of "The Nun Who Feigned Madness."[5] The eponymous nun, we are told, "'never sat down at the table or partook of a particle of bread, but ... wiped up with a sponge the crumbs from the tables.'"[6] This nun was ridiculed and abused by the other nuns in the monastery, but she never became angry with them. This dynamic was altered by a visit to the monastery from Saint Piteroum, who was told by an angel that among them existed "someone more pious than himself." After the sisters learn of her extraordinary piety, they confess to their maltreatment of her and begin to treat her as their "spiritual mother." "Unable to bear the praise and honors of the sisters," the nun disappeared from the monastery, and "nothing more of her was ever known." Barthes instructs us that the lesson of this tale is "be a fool, so that you may be wise." I suggest that we may understand this as a directive to allow oneself to be duped—to be taken in by the fiction of the Symbolic order.

To understand better the radical political possibilities implicit in this apparently conservative political strategy of allowing oneself to be duped, we must make a distinction between two sorts of subjects. On the one hand, after the revelation by St. Piteroum, the nuns in Palladius's text exemplify the position of the cynical nonduped who "see through" the parade of the nun's madness to her concealed sacred status, and thus refuse to be taken in by the Symbolic order's deceitful rejection of her. To put it in Barthes's terms, by rejecting the inherent duplicity of the Symbolic order, the "mad" suffer by refusing to "be fools." In Žižek's words, "with a disarming frankness [the cynical subject] 'admits everything' ... 'they know very well what they are doing, yet they are doing it.'"[7] The cynic is blinded to the fact that his or her ability to see through to how things "really are" matters very little, indeed merely preserves the status quo. On the other hand, for Barthes, the fool or the dupe is wise, because by allowing herself to be duped, she avoids the trap of believing that she can outsmart the efficiency of the symbolic ruse. In other words, the subject who allows herself to be duped, who avoids the possibility of believing she can step outside the illusion, inhabits the truth that, deceitful or not, it is the symbolic fiction that structures reality. In Lacanian parlance, one might say that it is by refusing to be fooled by the big Other that one falls into the errant trap of the "non-duped."

The duped engage in an inverse form of disavowal: the duped invest in the symbolic fiction—allow themselves to be taken in by the Other, even if it contradicts what they know. To be specific, for the duped, it does not matter if the nun is indeed the holiest among them: as long as she wears a rag on her head and mops up all the crumbs, she is the "reject." My suggestion, then, is that, despite its apparent conservatism, this scenario holds interesting possibilities for a radical politics.

Chapter 1, for example, demonstrates how we might arrive at an aesthetic politics, not by sidestepping the symbolic framework of the museum, but rather by committing to the efficaciousness of its artificial (symbolic) authority. I suggested that, by doubling the ruse, Ron Mueck's work facilitates an encounter with the constitutive nature of language. Mark Jenkins's work appeals to the logic of the nonduped subject, who, after an initial moment of uncertainty, can enjoy with confidence that reality is safely intact. The "reality testing" provoked by Jenkins's work resolves into an affirmative verdict for the maintenance of the status quo. Mueck's work, by contrast, lures spectators into an illusion that challenges them to question the symbolic system's guarantee that fiction and reality can be unequivocally adjudicated. But rather than entering into a Baudrillardian simulation, which risks being mistaken for (and/or claimed on behalf of) conventional reality, Mueck's work fails to resolve clearly into either "reality" or "fiction." In Rancièrian terms, we may say that, by foregrounding the inherent tensions within the realist form, Mueck unsettles the representative regime within which the realist form has traditionally been deployed. His work helps point to ways in which realism may contribute to a political aesthetic project.

In the films *Catfish* and *This Is Not a Film*, which I discuss in Chapter 2, we see again how fiction gives rise to the truth. *Catfish* exploits the realist conventions that lend credibility to the documentary form in a way that not only demonstrates the commonplace expectation that what is presented as truth might turn out to be a fiction but also shows the more radical possibility that fiction may pave the pathway for arriving at truth. The filmmakers appear to enact the logic of the nonduped by seeking to uncover the truth behind Angela's deception. But it soon becomes clear that by entering into the realm of deception themselves, they create ruptures in the symbolic framework of reality that give way to encounters with the Real. This framework helps explain the seemingly paradoxical terms used in A.O. Scott's review of the film in *The New York Times*: "untrustworthy and strangely authentic."[8] More than that, not only do the filmmakers and Nev undertake an untrustworthy pursuit of their own in response to Angela's deceit, they also position their own quest on the same representational plane as they do Angela's enterprise. In this sense, the film carries out a

Rancièrian disturbance by refusing to make the expected adjustments to aesthetic form in response to the imagined suitability of the subjects represented. *Catfish*, I argued, accomplishes what can be seen as a radically democratic move in Rancière's sense by including Angela and her family on the same representational plane as Nev and the filmmakers. Through the filmic presumption of equality, Angela, I contended, achieves representational parity (if not privilege) and succeeds in challenging the usual hierarchy that governs visibility.

This Is Not a Film displays a similar insight. Panahi begins the film as if he can occupy the position of the nonduped: he seeks to work around the representational impasse preventing him from making films by having a friend record him while he "tells" about his film rather than makes his film. Panahi breaks down in despair when the recognition of the impossibility of evading the representational sanction becomes acute. He cannot go on when he confronts that the constraint under which he operates is not simply the one imposed on him by the Iranian government but is rather a constitutive constraint, one that emerges from the impossibility of reaching the truth from outside the symbolic fiction. It is then that he occupies the "wise" position of duped and turns to his fiction films to point out how they give rise to the real. Along Rancièrian lines, we see that Panahi enacts a challenge to perceptual system from which he is barred.

In the case of Aliza Shvarts's Yale art project, addressed in Chapter 3, we encounter an artwork which falls short of intervening into the symbolic fiction to arrive at the truth. Shvartz rhetorically enacted the conservative position of the nonduped who sought to reveal the truth behind the institution's flimsy justification for prohibiting the display of her work. Rather than incite the transgressive potential of a "true" simulation, in Baudrillard's sense, Shvartz's piece merely upheld the Symbolic order.

Upon later reflection, however, Shvartz acknowledges the error in attempting to outsmart the "cruel" efficiency of the Symbolic ruse. She ruminates on the missed opportunity to position her work within the terms of the symbolic fiction that structures reality, rather than seeking to critique it from the outside. This possibility follows the logic of the duped who invest in the symbolic fiction, indeed, allow themselves to be taken in by the Other, in order to arrive at the contours of the Real, to which the symbolic fiction gives rise. In this way we can frame Shvartz's position in terms of Rancière's stance that one cannot aim to steer the effect of a work of art toward a particular reaction, but can only seek to create a space for making existing structures of intelligibility untenable.

Christoph Schlingensief's *Please Love Austria*, addressed in Chapter 4, provides us with an opportunity to encounter an aesthetic intervention that works against the possibility of inhabiting the position of the nonduped. Rather than offer a clear stance on asylum seekers in Austria for spectators to oppose or endorse, Schlingensief's "fiction" draws us into the Real of the antagonism. Through entering into the fiction, we encounter the "lie" at the core of the concept of inclusive democracy: namely, that democracy itself depends on exclusions. A more traditionally political project may seek to give voice and representational privilege to those who have been marginalized within a system. Schlingensief's piece, by contrast, highlights the ways in which democracy requires the exclusions it professes to deny. In complicating traditional approaches to multicultural representations, such as those that appeared in by *Sächsische Zeitung* and *Time* magazine, Schlingensief's work creates an antagonism, facilitating a space for a radical democratic project.

In Chapter 5, through an exploration of *The Joe Schmo Show*, we consider how a parody of a "reality" show might, unwittingly, bring spectators closer to the Real. By including viewers in the ruse perpetuated against Matt, the show provides spectators with an extraordinarily powerful vantage point of the nonduped. Yet the possibility of confidently maintaining this position is compromised by unexpected contingencies within the show. The more certain viewers are that they are safely in the know, the more they go astray. I suggested that this phenomenon of relishing the position of the duped, rather than trying to overcome it, may facilitate the potentially disruptive spectatorship position of woman.

Chapter 6 compared Wim Delvoye's art installation, the eating, digesting, excreting machine, *Cloaca*, and Gunther von Hagens's display of preserved human corpses, *Bodyworlds*. Although *Bodyworlds* appears to confront spectators with a disturbing encounter with "the living dead," I argued that it functions instead to offer a comforting fantasy of the dead living; it works to support the illusion that we can survive our own death. By contrast, *Cloaca*, apparently an amusing oddity, facilitates an unsettling response among spectators. The fictional, parodic, and humorous framework surrounding *Cloaca* not only fails to insulate it from creating anxiety but also works to create discomfort. By erecting a discourse of mastery, the viewer finds herself facing the Real in the guise of a fiction.

Chapter 7 considered the ways in which competing discourses surrounding contemporary, Western breastfeeding advocacy have been limited, due to their underappreciation of the dimension of the Real. The Real, which I suggest plays a significant role in one's relationship to the practice of breastfeeding, can only be encountered if one occupies the position of the duped, by acting in accordance with what lies beyond the rationality and sentimentality offered by the discourse of those who claim to not be duped. In this way, we can consider in a new light the controversy sparked by Hanna Rosin's provocative essay in *The Atlantic*, in which she, as a long-term breastfeeding mother, challenges the rhetoric of "breast is best." Perhaps Rosin's piece created a disturbance because in probing her desire to breastfeed, it points to the limitations of both the Imaginary fantasy of mother–child unity and the rational, scientific discourse of the nonduped. By disrupting both of these frameworks—the scientific (Symbolic) and the sentimental (Imaginary)—her article initiated a Rancièrian dissensus in which the oft-overlooked dimension played by the Real came to light.

Last, through an exploration of Lars von Trier's film *Melancholia*, we encountered the ways in which our supporting link to reality is maintained through the acceptance of illusion. In embracing the explicit fiction of the magic cave, Justine offers us insight into how one can live in the face of profound loss. Justine demonstrates the Lacanian position of woman by refusing the totalizing exception, and, by contrast, occupying the impossibility, which brings to the scene the truth of the Real.

NOTES

INTRODUCTION
1. Jacques Rancière, *The Emancipated Spectator*, trans. Gregory Elliott (London: Verso, 2009), 105.
2. Jacques Rancière, *Politics of Aesthetics*, trans. and introduction by Gabriel Rockhill (London: Continuum, 2006), 49.
3. Ibid.
4. Slavoj Žižek, *Interrogating the Real*, ed. Rex Butler and Scott Stephens (New York: Continuum, 2005), 23.
5. Rancière, *Emancipated Spectator*, 105.
6. Slavoj Žižek, *Plague of Fantasies* (London: Verso, 1997), 21.
7. Slavoj Žižek, *The Sublime Object of Ideology* (London: Verso, 1989), 33.
8. Rancière, *Politics of Aesthetics*, trans. and with introduction by Gabriel Rockhill (London: Continuum, 2006), 36.
9. Ibid., 39.
10. Alenka Zupančič, "Realism in Psychoanalysis," *European Journal of Psychoanalysis* 32 (2011): 32.
11. I am grateful to Jodi Dean for bringing the important work of Not an Alternative to my attention.
12. James F. Lastra, "Why Is This Absurd Picture Here? Ethnology/Heterology/Buñuel," in *Rites of Realism*, edited by Ivone Margulies (Durham, NC: Duke University Press, 2003), 187.
13. Ibid.
14. *Jacques Lacan, The Four Fundamental Concepts of Psychoanalysis: The Seminar of Jacques Lacan, Book XI*, ed. Jacques-Alain Miller, trans. Alan Sheridan (New York: Norton, 1998), 112.
15. Richard Allen, *Projecting Illusion: Film Spectatorship and the Impression of Reality* (Cambridge: Cambridge University Press, 1997), 82.
16. Brian Massumi, *Realer Than Real: The Simulacrum According to Deleuze and Guattari*," http://www.brianmassumi.com/textes/REALERTHANREAL.pdf.2.
17. Ibid., 1.
18. Richard Allen, *Projecting Illusion: Film Spectatorship and the Impression of Reality* (Cambridge: Cambridge University Press, 1997), 82.
19. Jean Baudrillard, *The Conspiracy of Art: Manifestos, Interviews, Essays* (New York, NY: Semiotext(e), 2005), 114.
20. Ibid., 118.
21. Ibid., 113.

22. Ibid., 113.
23. Ibid., 113.
24. Naomi Schor, *Reading in Detail: Aesthetics and the Feminine* (London: Routledge, 2007), 165.
25. Rancière, *Emancipated Spectator*, 9.
26. Barbara Creed, *Media Matrix: Sexing the New Reality* (Crowns Nest, NSW: Australia: Allen & Unwin, 2003), 2.
27. Ibid., 2.
28. Ibid., 2.
29. Jean Baudrillard, "Simulacra and Simulations," *Selected Writings*, ed. Mark Poster (Stanford, CA: Stanford University Press, 1988), 2. http://www.georgetown.edu/faculty/irvinem/CCTP738/sources/Baudrillard_Simulacra_and_Simulations.html.
30. Quoted in Matthew Beaumont, *A Concise Companion to Realism* (Malden, MA: Wiley-Blackwell, 2010), 7.
31. Rancière, *Emancipated Spectator*, 80.
32. Ibid., 101.

CHAPTER 1

1. Jacques Rancière, *Aesthetics and Its Discontents*, translated by Steven Corcoran (London: Polity, 2009), 25.
2. Rancière, *Emancipated Spectator*, 105.
3. Rancière, *Future of the Image*, 13.
4. Rancière, *Emancipated Spectator*, 121.
5. Rancière, *Future of the Image*, 13.
6. Rancière, *Politics of Aesthetics*, 12.
7. The examples interwoven throughout the piece are intended to go beyond merely providing aesthetic objects on which to ground abstract ideas. They aim, rather, to function as what Robert Pfaller calls "theoretical tools" in their own right—not just passive textual objects to be illuminated by a set of theoretical apparatuses but instead active devices for shedding new light on theoretical formulations. Robert Pfaller, "Why Žižek?—Interpassivity and Misdemeanours: The Analysis of Ideology and the Žižekian Toolbox," *International Journal of Žižek Studies* 1, no. 1 (2007): 33–50, http://Žižekstudies.org/index.pho/ijzs/article/view/19/69.
8. Susana Greeves, "A Redefinition of Realism," in *Ron Mueck*, edited by Heiner Bastian (Berlin: Hatje Cantz, 2006), 33.
9. Naomi Schor, *Reading in Detail: Aesthetics and the Feminine* (London: Routledge, 2007), 170.
10. Slavoj Žižek, *Plague of Fantasies* (London: Verso, 1997), 107.
11. Ibid.
12. Žižek, *Plague of Fantasies*, 107–108.
13. Slavoj Žižek, *In Defense of Lost Causes* (London: Verso, 2009), 300.
14. Žižek, *Plague of Fantasies*, 106.
15. Žižek, *Defense of Lost Causes*, 34. In support of his proclamation regarding the ubiquity of the big Other, Žižek explains that "The more one wants to be an atomist [live as if there is no big O regulating one's actions], the more some figure of the big Other is needed to regulate one's distance from others" (35). This point resonates with my own presumably not uncommon yet seemingly paradoxical need to be around others in order to "be alone." When I really

want to be alone, I must go out to a café by myself so that my "aloneness" can become officially registered in the eyes of the big Other/the social system. Such validation, of course, is a fiction, since as Joan Copjec depressingly reminds us, "Lacan does not ask you to think of the gaze as belonging to an Other who cares about what or who you are, who pries, keeps tabs on your whereabouts, and takes note of your steps and missteps, as the panoptic gaze is said to do. . . . So, if you are looking for confirmation of the truth of your being or the clarity of your vision, you are on your own; the gaze of the Other is not confirming; it will not validate you." Joan Copjec, *Read My Desire: Lacan Against the Historicists* (Cambridge, MA: MIT Press, 1994), 36.
16. Žižek, *Defense of Lost Causes*, 35.
17. Jacques Lacan, *Ecrits: A Selection Psychoanalysis,* translated by Alan Sheridan (New York: Norton 1997), 288.
18. Susan Bordo, *The Male Body: A New Look at Men in Public and in Private* (New York: Farrar, Straus and Giroux, 2000), 95.
19. Jean Baudrillard, "Simulacra and Simulations," in *Jean Baudrillard: Selected Writings*, edited by Mark Poster (Stanford, CA: Stanford University Press, 1988), 168.
20. Žižek, "The Interpassive Subject," *Traverses* (1998), www.lacan.com/Žižek-pompidou.htm.
21. Baudrillard, "Simulacra and Simulations," 144.
22. This scene, of course, implicitly cites Woody Allen's *Deconstructing Harry* (1997) in which Robin Williams plays an actor who becomes intradiegetically blurry and out of focus.
23. Lacan, *Four Fundamental*, 60.
24. Ibid., 106.
25. Rancière, *Future of the Image*, 137.
26. Heiner Bastian, "On Several Sculptures by Ron Mueck," in *Ron Mueck*, edited by Heiner Bastian (Berlin: Hatje Cantz Publishers, 2006), 62.
27. Greeves, "A Redefinition of Realism," 39.
28. Arthur Danto, "The Artworld," *Journal of Philosophy* 61, no. 19 (1964): 581.
29. Ibid., 581.
30. Schor, *Reading in Detail*, 173.
31. Ibid., 171.

CHAPTER 2
1. Rancière, *Politics of Aesthetics*, 53; *Future of the Image*, 12.
2. Rancière, *Future of the Image*, 13.
3. Ibid., 101.
4. Rancière, *Aesthetics and Its Discontents*, 25.
5. Rancière, *Future of the Image*, 106.
6. Žižek, *Tarrying with the Negative: Kant, Hegel, and the Critique of Ideology* (Durham, NC: Duke University Press, 1993), 91.
7. Scott Hutcheson, "CATFISH: Real or Fake? It's a Fake . . . Sort of," catfishfans.com, http://veryaware.com/2010/09/catfish-real-or-fake-its-a-fake-sort-of/.
8. Tracie Egan Morrissey, "*Catfish* Filmmakers Get the Third Degree," http://jezebel.com/5661158/catfish-filmmakers-get-the-third-degree,10/11/10.
9. Olivia Solon, "Catfish Review and Interview with Nev Schulman," *Wired*, http://www.wired.co.uk/news/archive/2010-12/10/catfish-review-and-interview?page=all.

10. Josh Ralske, "Review" http://www.allmovie.com/movie/catfish-v507353/review
11. Rancière, *Emancipated Spectator*, 103.
12. Rancière, *Future of the Image*, 118.
13. Rancière, *Politics of Aesthetics*, 1.
14. Rancière, *Aesthetics and Its Discontents*, 25.
15. Rancière, *Politics of Aesthetics*, 32.
16. Rancière, *Future of the Image*, 120–121.
17. Thus, *Catfish* enacts the democratic premise elaborated by Rancière in *The Ignorant School Master*: the presumption of equality creates equality. By implicitly taking equality for granted— through ceding unadjusted power of representation to Angela—*Catfish* undermines the hierarchy implied by the conventional documentary form.
18. A representative comment along these lines comes from one on-line discussant who claims that Angela's "ego" "overrid[es] any shame or embarrassment that a normal person would experience." *Catfish: Why the 'Hoax' Is Probably Fake*, http://www.rowthree.com/2010/10/22/catfish-why-the-hoax-is-probably-fake/.
19. Although Rancière's framework does not base the success of an aesthetic politics on its effects, it might nonetheless be worth noting that Angela's visibility as an artist soared after the film. As a reporter for a local Michigan newspaper attests, "Pierce's art ended up on display in a sold-out exhibit in New York City after the documentary made its debut. And she was commissioned to do paintings by people across the globe." Renee Prusi, "Thrilled to Be Chosen: Pierce Happy to Be Part of Local Art Exhibit," *Miningjournal*, http://www.miningjournal.net/page/content.detail/id/563668/Thrilled-to-be-chosen.html.
20. Rancière, *Politics of Aesthetics*, 63.
21. Slavoj Žižek, *Der Ärger mit dem Realen* [Troubles with the Real] (Vienna: Sonderzahl, 2008), 78.
22. Rancière, *Future of the Image*, 109.
23. Ibid., 137.
24. Ibid., 112.
25. Slavoj Žižek, *The Fright of Real Tears: Krzysztof Kieslowski Between Theory and Post-Theory* (London: BFI Publishing, 2001), 71.
26. Rancière, *Future of the Image*, 126.
27. Ibid., 123; italics added.
28. "Jacques-Rancière Interview 2007," *Void Manufacturing*, http://voidmanufacturing.wordpress.com/2008/10/15/jacques-Rancière-interview-2007.
29. Rancière, *Politics of Aesthetics*, 35.
30. After the completion of the film, Panahi's appeal of his six-year prison sentence was denied and his colleague on the film, Mirtahmasb, "was detained in Tehran on his way to Toronto for the North American première of the collaboration. After three months in prison, Mirtahmasb was released." Karina Longworth, "*This Is Not a Film*: Jafar Panahi Is a Filmmaker Who Isn't," http://www.phoenixnewtimes.com/movies/this-is-not-a-film-in-film-nist-6709885.
31. Daniel Kasman, "Notebook Review: Jafar Panahi and Mojtaba Mirtahmasb's 'This Is Not a Film,'" https://mubi.com/notebook/posts/notebook-reviews-jafar-panahi-and-mojtaba-mirtahmasbs-this-is-not-a-film.
32. Ivonne Marguilies, "Bodies Too Much," *Rites of Realism*, ed. Ivone Marguilies (Durham, NC: Duke University Press, 2003), 3–4.
33. Ibid., 37.

34. Post-Gazette.Com, "'Catfish' Swears It's All True," http://www.post-gazette.com/pg/10274/1091655-60.stm.
35. Rebecca Milzroff, "Can You Believe This?" *NY Magazine,* http://nymag.com/movies/features/68100/.
36. Nichols, 38.
37. Ibid., 57, 62.
38. Ibid., 60.
39. Milzroff, "Can You Believe This?"
40. Ibid.
41. Žižek, *Fright of Real Tears,* 77.
42. Scott Hutcheson, "CATFISH: Real or Fake? It's a Fake . . . Sort of." catfishfans.com, http://veryaware.com/2010/09/catfish-real-or-fake-its-a-fake-sort-of/.
43. Another component that impedes the film's realist credentials involves its use of technology. The film faces the unusual challenge of claiming to truthfully document a deception by using the same media that were used to perpetuate deception. If they successfully demonstrate that they were taken in by the clever sham, then viewers are understandably encouraged to doubt whether they, too, are prey to a similarly devious deployment of technology.
44. Philip Rosen, "History of Image, Image of History: Subject and Ontology in Bazin," in *Rites of Realism,* ed. Ivone Margulies (Durham, NC: Duke University Press, 2002), 58.
45. Žižek, *Fright of Real Tears,* 75.
46. Cath Clarke, "Review of *This Is Not a Film,*" *Time Out London,* http://www.timeout.com/film/reviews/90841/this-is-not-a-film.html.
47. Žižek, *Fright of Real Tears,* 75.
48. Rancière, *Politics of Aesthetics,* 38.
49. Tom Conley, "Cinema and Its Discontents: Jacques Rancière and Film Theory," *SubStance* 34, no. 3 (2005), 96.
50. John Frosch, "Banned Iranian Director Jafar Panahi Makes a Movie, and a Statement," http://www.france24.com/en/20110926-banned-iranian-director-jafar-panahi-makes-movie-statement-this-is-not-a-film-mirtahmasb.
51. Rancière, *Politics of Aesthetics,* 63.
52. André Bazin, "Death Every Afternoon," *Rites of Realism,* ed. Ivone Margulies (Durham, NC: Duke University Press, 2002), 31.
53. George Kouvaros, "'We Do Not Die Twice': Realism and Cinema," *The SAGE Handbook of Film Studies* (London: SAGE Publications, 2008).
54. Siegfried Kracauer, *Theory of Film: The Redemption of Physical Reality* (Princeton, NJ: Princeton University Press, 1997), xxv.
55. Conley, "Cinema and Its Discontents," 103.

CHAPTER 3

1. "Aliza Shvarts' Insists Miscarriage Art Project Is Real," *Huffpost Health Living,* http:// www.huffingtonpost.com/ 2008/ 04/ 17/ yale- student- artificially_ n_ 97194.html.
2. Ibid.
3. "Shvartz, Yale Clash over Project," Yaledailynews.com, http://yaledailynews.com/blog/2008/04/18/shwartz-yale-clash-over-project/.
4. Jacques Lacan, *Ecrits: A Selection,* trans. Alan Sheridan (New York: Tavistock, 1977), 305.
5. Žižek, *Plague of Fantasies,* 36.

6. Jezebel.com, "One Thing Is Certain: Right Now, Yale University & Aliza Shvarts '08 Are 100% Annoying," http://jezebel.com/381279/one-thing-is-certain-right-now-yale-university--aliza-shvarts-08-are-100-annoying.
7. Jean Baudrillard, *Selected Writings*, ed. Mark Poster (Stanford, CA: Stanford University, 2001), 163.
8. Ibid., 180.
9. Ibid.
10. Ibid., 182.
11. Brian Massumi, "*Realer Than Real: The Simulacrum According to Deleuze and Guattari*," http://www.brianmassumi.com/textes/REALERTHANREAL.pdf.
12. Paul Verhaeghe, *Beyond Gender: From Subject to Drive* (New York: Other Press, 2001), 39.
13. Quoted in Martine Powers, "Shwartz, Yale Clash."
14. Ibid.
15. Jacques Rancière, *The Intervals of Cinema* Paper, trans. John Howe (London: Verso, 2014), 128, 130.
16. Rancière, *Politics of Aesthetics*, 63.

CHAPTER 4

1. Ibid., 3.
2. Lapsley and Westlake, *Film Theory: An Introduction* (Manchester: Manchester University Press, 1988), 163.
3. Žižek, *Fright of Real Tears*, 77.
4. Žižek, *Sublime Object*, 190.
5. Lukács, *Essays on Realism*, ed. Rodney Livingstone, trans. David Fernbach (Cambridge, MA: MIT Press, 1981), 51.
6. Ibid., 57.
7. Ibid., 58.
8. Ibid., 57.
9. Bitzan, "Please Love Austria." CommonSense 2000–2001. http://www.cs-journal.org/111/II1pspolitics2.html.
10. Laurie Ouellette, "'Take Responsibility for Yourself': *Judge Judy* and the Neoliberal Citizen," in *Reality TV: Remaking Television Culture*, ed. Susan Murray and Laurie Ouellette (New York: New York University Press, 2004), 232.
11. Ibid.
12. Mark Rectanus, *Culture Incorporated: Museums, Artists, and Corporate Sponsorships* (Minneapolis: University of Minnesota Press, 2002), 84.
13. Victor Burgin, *In/Different Spaces: Place and Memory in Visual Culture* (Los Angeles: University of California Press, 1996), 259.
14. Ibid., 260.
15. Ibid.
16. Žižek, *Fright of Real Tears*, 65.
17. MacCabe "Riviera Eschatology," 140–141.
18. Claire Bishop, "Participation and Spectacle: Where Are We Now?"*Living As Form: Socially Engaged Art from 1991–2011*, ed. Nato Thompson (Cambridge, MA: MIT Press, 2012), 45.
19. Stuart Hall, here, is describing the relationship between cultural studies theory and politics, but I am adapting his position to speak to the relationship of art to politics.

20. Stuart Hall, *Stuart Hall: Critical Dialogues in Cultural Studies* (New York: Routledge, 1996), 272.
21. Rosalyn Deutsche. "Art and Public Space: Questions of Democracy," *Social Text* 33 (1992), 35.

CHAPTER 5

1. Tania Modleski, *The Women Who Knew Too Much: Hitchcock and Feminist Theory* (New York: Routledge, 1988), 6; italics added.
2. Barbara Creed, *Media Matrix: Sexing the New Reality* (Crowns Nest, NSW: Australia: Allen & Unwin), 2003, 37.
3. Ibid., 40.
4. "Saving Private Lynch Story 'Flawed,'" BBC News, http://news.bbc.co.uk/1/hi/programmes/correspondent/3028585.stm.
5. Rob Owen, "Jessica Lynch Movie," Post-gazette.com, http://old.post-gazette.com/tv/20030710owen0710fnp2.asp.
6. "The Reagans" aired at the end of November on CBS's sister station, Showtime, to one-fifth of the expected audience.
7. Žižek, *Plague of Fantasies*, 21.
8. This chapter deals solely with the first season of the show, whose first episode aired September 2, 2003. *The Joe Schmo Show* was followed by *The Joe Schmo Show II*, which premiered June 15, 2004. Rather than continue its parody of the *Big Brother*–style show, this second incarnation involved both a male and a female "schmo" in spoofing the genre of reality TV dating shows, most notably, *The Bachelor*. After just a few episodes the female "schmo" caught on that the show was a hoax, a suspicion the producers confirmed. She was then invited to join the cast of actors who would perpetuate the ruse on her (still unsuspecting) male counterpart and a new female "schmo" was selected to take her place.
9. *The Joe Schmo Show*, directed by Danny Salles (2004).
10. Allspark.COMmunity, http://boards.allspark.com/index.php?showtopic=31089.
11. *The Joe Schmo Show*.
12. Frazierhome, http://www.frazierhome.net/node/view/226.
13. "'Joe Schmo' Duped in New Reality Show."
14. Rancière, *Politics of Aesthetics*, 63.
15. Randy Laist, "The Hyperreal Theme in 1990s American Cinema," *Americana: The Journal of American Popular Culture (1990-present)* 9, no. 1 (2010): par. 10, http://www.americanpopularculture.com/journal/articles/spring_2010/laist.htm.
16. Kevin Fallon, "How 'UnREAL' Became Summer's Best TV Show," http://www.thedailybeast.com/articles/2015/08/03/how-unreal-became-summer-s-best-tv-show.html).
17. Rebecca Nicholson, "Could Dark Dating-Show Satire *UnReal* Kill Reality TV?" http://www.theguardian.com/tv-and-radio/tvandradioblog/2015/jul/14/could-dark-dating-show-satire-unreal-kill-reality-tv.
18. Ibid.
19. I offer a detailed engagement with sexuation and spectatorship in *Feminine Look: Spectatorship, Sexuation, Subversion* (New York: SUNY Press, 2009). The following discussion draws upon this work.
20. Jacqueline Rose, *In the Field of Vision* (London: Verso, 1986), 231.
21. Ellie Ragland-Sullivan, "The Sexual Masquerade: A Lacanian Theory of Sexual Difference," in *Lacan and the Subject of Language*, ed. Ellie Ragland-Sullivan and Mark Bracher (New York: Routledge, 1991), 75.

22. Rose, *Sexuality*, 219.
23. Elizabeth Cowie, *Representing the Woman: Cinema and Psychoanalysis* (London: Macmillan, 1997), 288.

CHAPTER 6
1. Els Fiers, "A Human Masterpiece," http://www.artnet.com/magazine/reviews/fiers/fiers1-9-01.asp.
2. Much controversy surrounds the question of the provenance of the bodies obtained by Von Hagens. He faces frequent accusations that some of the bodies he uses are those of executed political prisoners from China. In 2004 von Hagens admitted having discovered bullet wounds in the heads of some bodies and had seven corpses returned to China for burial. (Luke Harding, "Von Hagens Forced to Return Controversial Corpses to China," *The Guardian*, http://www.theguardian.com/world/2004/jan/23/arts.china)
3. Information packet accompanying exhibit 27.
4. Julia Kristeva, *Powers of Horror: An Essay on Abjection* (New York: Columbia University Press, 1982), 71.
5. Ibid., 71.
6. Ibid., 4.
7. Ibid., 3.
8. Ibid., 3–4.
9. Miran Božovič, "The Body and Psycho; or, of 'Farther Uses of the Dead to the Living,'" *Umbr(a)*, no. 1 (2000): 86.
10. Wim Delvoye, interview by Josefina Ayerza, http://www.lacan.com/lacinkXIX7.htm.
11. Hal Foster, *Return of the Real* (Cambridge, MA: MIT Press, 1996), 164.
12. Lacan, *Four Fundamental*, 73.
13. Sean Homer, *Jacques Lacan* (London: Routledge, 2005), 22.
14. Denis Hollier and William Rodarmor, "Mimesis and Castration," *October* 31 (1984): 12–13.
15. Lacan, *Four Fundamental*, 99.
16. Ibid., 13.
17. Žižek, *Sublime Object*, 76.
18. Lacan, *Four Fundamental*, 207.
19. Ibid., 218.
20. Ibid., 43.
21. Jacques, Lacan, *Ecrits: A Selection*, trans. Alan Sheridan (New York: Tavistock, 1977), 152.
22. Jacques-Alain Miller, "The Symptom and the Body Event," trans. Barbara P. Fulks, *Lacanian Ink* 19 (2001): 35.
23. Ibid.
24. Vivian Sobchack, *The Address of the Eye: A Phenomenology of Film Experience* (Princeton, NJ: Princeton University Press, 1992), 120.
25. Delvoye, interview, http://www.lacan.com/lacinkXIX7.htm.
26. Lynda Hart, *Between the Body and the Flesh: Performing Sadomasochism* (New York: Columbia University Press, 1998), 86.
27. Žižek Slavoj, *Organs Without Bodies: Deleuze and Consequences* (New York: Routledge, 2004), 65.
28. Zupančič, "Realism in Psychoanalysis," *European Journal of Psychoanalysis* 32 (2011): 32.

29. Žižek Slavoj, *In Defense of Lost Causes* (London: Verso, 2009), 321.
30. Lacan, *Four Fundamental*, 50.
31. Roberto Harari, *Lacan's Seminar on Anxiety: An Introduction* (New York: Other Press 2001), 97.
32. Lacan, *Four Fundamental*, 54.
33. Ibid., 104.
34. Žižek, *In Defense*, 320.
35. Homi Bhabha, *The Location of Culture* (New York: Routledge, 1994), 86.
36. Ibid.
37. Ibid., 91.
38. Ibid.
39. Harari, *Lacan's Seminar*, 139.
40. Lacan, *Anxiety*, 302.
41. Žižek, *Organs*, 127.
42. Lacan, *Four Fundamental*, 184.
43. Jessica Riskin, "The Defecating Duck, Or, The Ambiguous Origins of Artificial Life," *Critical Inquiry* 20, no. 4 (Summer 2003), 601.
44. Ibid., 599.
45. Ibid., 606.
46. Ibid., 610, 612.
47. Ibid., 613.
48. Ibid.
49. Wim Delvoye, "Wim Delvoye: Cloaca 2000–2007," http://we-make-money-not-art.com/archives/2008/01/wim-delvoye-cloaca-20002007.php.
50. Jonathan Glancey, "Merde d'artiste: Not Exactly What It Says on the Tin," *The Guardian*, http://www.theguardian.com/artanddesign/2007/jun/13/art.
51. Holland Cotter, "To Bump Off Art as He Knew It" *The New York Times*, February 12, 2009.
52. Sophie Howarth, "Piero Manzoni: Artist's Shit 1961," http://www.tate.org.uk/art/artworks/manzoni-artists-shit-t07667/text-summary.
53. Žižek, *Plague of Fantasies*, 36.
54. Todd McGowan's *The Fictional Christopher Nolan* provides an outstanding account of the "ontological primacy of the lie." Todd McGowan, *The Fictional Christopher Nolan* (Austin: University of Texas Press, 2012), 1.
55. Vladimir Safatle, "Mirrors Without Images: Mimesis and Recognition in Lacan and Adorno," http://www.oocities.org/vladimirsafatle/vladi089.htm.

CHAPTER 7

1. Hannah Rosin, "The Case Against Breast-Feeding," *The Atlantic*, http://www.theatlantic.com.
2. Ibid.
3. It is also worth noting that within Europe there is considerable variation in breastfeeding statistics, with Scandinavian countries engaging in near total conformity with governmental regulations for breastfeeding compliance and Ireland and France representing the lowest levels of breastfeeding compliance in Europe.
4. Badinter, *The Conflict: How Modern Motherhood Undermines the Status of Women* (New York: Metropolitan Books, 2011), 71–72.
5. Copjec, "Vampires," 28.
6. Ibid.

7. Rebecca Kukla, "Ethics and Ideology in Breastfeeding Advocacy Campaigns," *Hypatia* 21, no. 1 (2006), 160.
8. *Bébé Au Lait*.
9. Krips, "Mass Media," 6.
10. Ibid., 18–22.
11. Copjec, "Vampires," 28.
12. Ibid.
13. Žižek, *Sublime*, 164.
14. Žižek, "Introduction," in *Mapping Ideology*, ed. Slavoj Žižek (London: Verso, 1994), 7.
15. National Breastfeeding Awareness Campaign, http://www.womenshealth.gov/breastfeeding/?=Campaign.
16. Ibid.
17. Ibid.
18. Womenshealth, "Breastfeeding," http://womenshealth.gov/breastfeeding/breastfeeding-in-public/.
19. Bernice Hausman, "Things (Not) to Do with Breasts in Public: Maternal Embodiment and the Biocultural Politics of Infant Feeding," *New Literary History* 38, no. 3 (2007): 479–504.
20. Womenshealth, "Breastfeeding."
21. Hausman, "Things (Not)," 503.
22. Breastfeeding is permissible anywhere that a woman and her child are permitted to be. Several US states have put in place explicit provisions for protecting breastfeeding from public indecency laws, even if the nipple is exposed. This information is omitted from the narrative content of the government website, but they do provide links to these laws. It is perhaps noteworthy that the sites to which they direct us for this information are sponsored by La Leche League International.
23. Womenshealth, "Breastfeeding."
24. Le Leche League International, http://lalecheleague.org/
25. Linda Blum, *At the Breast: Ideologies of Breastfeeding and Motherhood in the Contemporary United States* (Boston: Beacon Press, 1999), 65.
26. Ibid.
27. Ibid.
28. Ibid., 53.
29. The national breastfeeding campaign minimizes the severe inadequacies of the Family and Medical Leave Act through the use of voluntaristic rhetoric. They blithely advise: "Take as many weeks off as you can. At least six weeks of leave can help you recover from childbirth and settle into a good breastfeeding routine. Twelve weeks is even better." Womenshealth, "Breastfeeding."
30. Hausman, "Things (Not)," 174–175.
31. Rosin, "Case Against Breast-Feeding."
32. *KellyMom Parenting Breastfeeding*, http://kellymom.com.
33. Ibid.
34. Blum, *At the Breast*, 53–55.
35. Adrian Johnston, "The Cynic's Fetish: Slavoj Žižek and the Dynamics of Belief," *Psychoanalysis, Culture, & Society* 9, no. 3 (2004): 264.
36. Ann Oakley alerts us to exactly this reality when she adds breastfeeding to her list of conditions of embodiment that she terms "two-in-one" bodies, such as

pregnancy and conjoined twins, which deliver a blow to the myth of bodily integrity.
37. Blum, *At the Breast*, 98, 66.
38. La Leche League, *The Womanly Art of Breast-feeding* (New York: Plume, 2004), quoted in Blum, *At the Breast*, 98.
39. Glyn Daly, "Risking the Impossible," http://www.lacan.com/Žižek-daly.htm (accessed December 12, 2012).
40. Copjec, "Vampires," 33.
41. Ibid., 34.
42. Mladen Dolar, "'I Shall Be with You on Your Wedding-Night': Lacan and the Uncanny," *October* 58 (1991): 6.
43. Žižek, "Truth Arises," 188.
44. Harari, *Lacan's Seminar*, 113.
45. Marie-Hélène Brousse, "Strange Objects, Immaterial Objects Why Does Lacan Include the Voice and the Gaze in the Series of Freudian Objects?" *International Lacanian Review*, para. 5, http://www.lacancircle.net/MHBStrangeobjects.pdf.
46. Harari, *Lacan's Seminar*, 190.
47. Lacan, *Four Fundamental*, 313.
48. Dolar, "'I Shall Be,'" 15.
49. Lapsley, *Film Theory*, 72.
50. Fink, *Lacanian Subject*, 103.
51. Verhaeghe, *Beyond Gender*, 38–39.

CHAPTER 8

1. Quoted in Marta Figlerowicz, "Comedy of Abandon: Lars von Trier's *Melancholia*," *Film Quarterly* 65, no. 4 (2012): 21–26.
2. Slavoj Žižek, "The Optimism of Melancholia," http:bigthink.com/videos/the-optimism-of-melancholia.
3. Steven Shaviro, "Melancholia or, the Romantic Anti-Sublime," *Sequence* 1, no. 1 (2012): 32–33, http://reframe.sussex.ac.uk/sequence/files/2012/12/MELANCHOLIA-or-The-Romantic-Anti-Sublime-SEQUENCE-1.1-2012-Steven-Shaviro.pdf.
4. Lacan, *Encore*, 79.
5. Shaviro, "Melancholia," 35.
6. John's suicide should be read as a response to his inability to face having been exposed as a fraud. Otherwise we are left with the less plausible explanation that he kills himself in order to avoid death.
7. And to this list of pathetic male characters, we might also add Justine and Claire's father. Rather than an impostor, he embodies the ineffectual father who fails to mobilize the symbolic law and for whom all women are interchangeable (and appear to him to all be named "Betty"). As the only man Justine turns to when she finds herself at her wedding utterly unable to cope with the façade of happiness required of the bride, he inexplicably abandons her.
8. I develop these strategies in more detail in *Feminine Look: Sexuation, Spectatorship, and Subversion* (New York: SUNY Press, 2008).
9. Christopher Peterson, "The Magic Cave of Allegory: Lars von Trier's *Melancholia*," *Discourse* 35, no. 3 (2013), 407.
10. Ibid., 402.
11. Ibid., 411.

12. Ibid., 412.
13. André Bazin, "Death Every Afternoon," 31.
14. Neil Maizels, "*Melancholia, Cosmolis*, and Modern Pain," http://www.academia.edu/4117527/Melancholia_and_Cosmopolis_Arena_Magazine.
15. Fink, *Lacanian Subject*, 64.
16. Žižek, *Sublime*, 69.
17. Ibid.
18. Peterson, "The Magic Cave of Allegory: Lars von Trier's *Melancholia*," *Discourse* 35, no. 3 (2013): 401.
19. Ibid., 403.
20. Sigmund Freud, "Inhibitions, Symptoms, and Anxiety," in *The Standard Edition of the Complete Psychological Works of Sigmund Freud, Vol. 20*, ed. James Strachey (London: Hogarth Press, 1925), 4315.
21. Ibid., 4315.
22. MacCabe, "Riviera Eschatology," 63.
23. Peterson, "The Magic Cave of Allegory: Lars von Trier's *Melancholia*," *Discourse* 35, no. 3 (2013): 401.
24. Žižek, "Melancholia," 658.
25. Lacan, *Anxiety*, 335.
26. Žižek, "Melancholia," 661.
27. Lacan, *Anxiety*, 333.
28. Freud, "Inhibitions," 169.
29. Ibid., 169.
30. Ibid., 166.
31. Ibid., 169.
32. Lacan, *Anxiety*, 54.
33. Ibid., 53.
34. Ibid.
35. Lacan, *Anxiety*, 76.
36. Ibid., 297.
37. Ibid., 231. It might be argued that deception arises within the formation of anxiety in an additional way. Although Lacan asserts that as an affect, anxiety never lies, "the signifiers that moor it" are unreliable as a result of the process of repression. Lacan, *Anxiety*, 14.
38. Ibid., 9.
39. Ibid., 77.
40. Ibid.
41. Ibid., 42.
42. Peterson, "The Magic Cave of Allegory: Lars von Trier's *Melancholia*," *Discourse* 35, no. 3 (2013): 407.
43. Slavoj Žižek, *On Belief* (New York: Routledge, 2001).
44. Lacan, *Anxiety*, 50.
45. Ibid.
46. Ibid., 49.
47. Ibid., 50.
48. Ibid., 51.
49. Ibid.
50. Steven Shaviro, "Melancholia," 44.
51. Ibid.
52. Maizels, "*Melancholia*," 23.

53. Shaviro, "Melancholia," 49.
54. Peterson, "The Magic Cave of Allegory: Lars von Trier's *Melancholia*," *Discourse* 35, no. 3 (2013): 415.
55. Zaha Zalloua, "Žižek with French Femnism: Enjoyment and the Feminine Logic of the 'Not-All.'" *Intertexts* 18, no. 2 (2014): 112–113.
56. Peterson, "The Magic Cave of Allegory: Lars von Trier's *Melancholia*," *Discourse* 35, no. 3 (2013): 419.
57. Ibid.
58. Žižek, *Plague*, 107–108.
59. Žižek, "Melancholia," 671.
60. Žižek, "Optimism."
61. Ibid.

CONCLUSION
1. Žižek, *How to Read Lacan* (New York: Norton, 2007), 33.
2. Žižek, *Interrogating*, 230.
3. Ibid., 232.
4. Ibid., 243.
5. Roland Barthes, *How to Live Together: Novelistic Simulations of Some Everyday Spaces*, trans. Kate Briggs (New York: Columbia University Press, 2012).
6. Ibid., 82.
7. Žižek, "Introduction," 8.
8. A.O. Scott, "The World Where You Aren't What You Post," http://www.nytimes.com/2010/09/17catfish.html?_r=0

BIBLIOGRAPHY

Allen, Richard. *Projecting Illusion: Film Spectatorship and the Impression of Reality.* Cambridge: Cambridge University Press, 1997
Allspark.COMmunity. http://boards.allspark.com/index.php?showtopic=31089.
Badinter, Elisabeth. *The Conflict: How Modern Motherhood Undermines the Status of Women.* New York: Metropolitan Books, 2011.
Barthes, Roland. *How to Live Together: Novelistic Simulations of Some Everyday Spaces.* Translated by Kate Briggs. New York: Columbia University Press, 2012.
Barthes, Roland. *Mythologies.* Translated by Annette Lavers. New York: Hill and Wang, 1972.
Baudrillard, Jean. *The Conspiracy of Art: Manifestos, Interviews, Essays.* New York, NY: Semiotext(e), 2005.
Baudrillard, Jean. *Selected Writings.* Edited by Mark Poster. Stanford, CA: Stanford University Press, 2001.
Bazin, André. "Death Every Afternoon." *Rites of Realism.* Edited by Ivone Margulies. Durham, NC: Duke University Press, 2002.
BBC News. "Saving Private Lynch Story 'Flawed.'" http://news.bbc.co.uk/1/hi/programmes/correspondent/3028585.stm.
Bébé Au Lait. http://www.bebeaulait.com/about-us/our-story.
Beaumont, Matthew. *A Concise Companion to Realism.* Malden, MA: Wiley-Blackwell, 2010.
Bhabha, Homi. *The Location of Culture.* London: Routledge, 1994.
Bishop, Claire. "Participation and Spectacle: Where Are We Now?" In *Living as Form: Socially Engaged Art from 1991–2011*, edited by Nato Thompson, 34–45. Cambridge, MA: MIT Press, 2012.
Bitzan, Amos. "Please Love Austria." CommonSense 2000–2001. http://www.cs-journal.org/111/II1pspolitics2.html.
Blum, Linda. *At the Breast: Ideologies of Breastfeeding and Motherhood in the Contemporary United States.* Boston: Beacon Press, 1999.
Božovič, Miran. "The Body and Psycho; or, of 'Farther Uses of the Dead to the Living.'" *Umbr(a)* no. 1 (2000): 81–98.
Broun, Alex. "Free the Refugees: Merlin Interviewed." *Green Left Weekly* 23, no. 586, June 23, 2004. http://www.greenleft.org.au/2004/586/32324.
Brousse, Marie-Hélène. "Strange Objects, Immaterial Objects Why Does Lacan Include the Voice and the Gaze in the Series of Freudian Objects?" *International Lacanian Review.* http://www.lacancircle.net/MHBStrangeobjects.pdf.

Burgin, Victor. *In/Different Spaces: Place and Memory in Visual Culture*. Los Angeles: University of California Press, 1996.

Catfish. Directed by Ariel Schulman and Henry Joost. 2010.

Catfishfans.com. "Catfish: Real or Fake? It's a Fake . . . Sort of." http://veryaware.com/2010/09/catfish-real-or-fake-its-a-fake-sort-of/).

Clarke, Cath. "Review of *This Is Not a Film*." *Time Out London*. March 29, 2012. http://www.timeout.com/film/reviews/90841/this-is-not-a-film.html.

CNN. "'Joe Schmo' Duped in New Reality Show." http://us.cnn.com/2003/SHOWBIZ/TV/08/29/television.joe.schmo.reut/.

Conley, Tom. "Cinema and Its Discontents: Jacques Rancière and Film Theory." *SubStance* 34, no. 3 (2005): 96–106.

Copjec, Joan. "Vampires, Breast-Feeding, and Anxiety." *October* 58 (1991): 25–43.

Cotter, Holland. "To Bump Off Art as He Knew It." *The New York Times*, February 12, 2009.

Cowie, Elizabeth. *Representing the Woman: Cinema and Psychoanalysis*. London: Macmillan, 1997.

Creed, Barbara. *Media Matrix: Sexing the New Reality*. Crowns Nest, NSW: Allen & Unwin, 2003.

Daly, Glyn. "Risking the Impossible." http://www.lacan.com/Žižek-daly.htm

Daney, Serge. "The Screen of Fantasy (Bazin and Animals)." Translated by Mark A. Cohen. *Rites of Realism*. Edited by Ivone Margulies. Durham, NC: Duke University Press, 2002.

Danto, Arthur. "The Artworld." *Journal of Philosophy* 61, no. 19 (1964): 571–584.

Delvoye, Wim. Interview by Josefina Ayerza. http://www.lacan.com/lacinkXIX7.htm.

Delvoye, Wim. "Wim Delvoye: Cloaca 2000–2007." http://we-make-money-not-art.com/archives/2008/01/wim-delvoye-cloaca-20002007.php.

Deutsche, Rosalyn. "Art and Public Space: Questions of Democracy." *Social Text* 33 (1992): 34–53.

Dolar, Mladen. "'I Shall Be with You on Your Wedding-Night': Lacan and the Uncanny." *October* 58 (1991): 5–23.

Eagleton, Terry. "Ideology and Its Vicissitudes in Western Marxism." *Mapping Ideology*. Edited by Slavoj Žižek. London: Verso, 1994.

Fallon, Kevin. "How 'UnREAL' Became Summer's Best TV Show." thedailybeast.com. http://www.thedailybeast.com/articles/2015/08/03/how-unreal-became-summer-s-best-tv-show.html.

Fiers, Els. "A Human Masterpiece." http://www.artnet.com/magazine/reviews/fiers/fiers1-9-01.asp.

Figlerowicz, Marta. "The Comedy of Abandon: Lars von Trier's *Melancholia*." *Film Quarterly* 65, no. 4 (2012): 21–26.

Fink, Bruce. *The Lacanian Subject: Between Language and Jouissance*. Princeton, NJ: Princeton University Press, 1995.

Foster, Hal. *Recordings: Art, Spectacle, Cultural Politics*. Seattle: Bay Press, 1985.

Foster, Hal. *Return of the Real*. Cambridge, MA: MIT Press, 1996. Frazierhome. http://www.frazierhome.net/node/view/226.

Freud, Sigmund. "Inhibitions, Symptoms, and Anxiety." In *The Standard Edition of the Complete Psychological Works of Sigmund Freud Vol. 20*, edited by James Strachey, 87–175. London: Hogarth Press, 1925.

Frosch, John. "Banned Iranian Director Jafar Panahi Makes a Movie, and a Statement." http://www.france24.com/en/20110926-banned-iranian-director-jafar-panahi-makes-movie-statement-this-is-not-a-film-mirtahmasb.

Glancey, Jonathan. "Merde d'artiste: Not Exactly What It Says on the Tin." *The Guardian*. http://www.theguardian.com/artanddesign/2007/jun/13/art.
Hall, Stuart. *Stuart Hall: Critical Dialogues in Cultural Studies*. New York: Routledge, 1996.
Hansen, Miriam. Introduction to Sigfried Kracauer's *Theory of Film: The Redemption of Physical Reality*. Princeton, NJ: Princeton University Press, 1997.
Harari, Roberto. *Lacan's Seminar on Anxiety: An Introduction*. New York: Other Press 2001.
Harding, Luke. "Von Hagens Forced to Return Controversial Corpses to China." *The Guardian*. http://www.theguardian.com/world/2004/jan/23/arts.china.
Hart, Lynda. *Between the Body and the Flesh: Performing Sadomasochism*. New York: Columbia University Press, 1998.
Hausman, Bernice. *Mother's Milk: Breastfeeding Controversies in American Culture*. New York: Routledge, 2003.
Hausman, Bernice. "Things (Not) to Do with Breasts in Public: Maternal Embodiment and the Biocultural Politics of Infant Feeding." *New Literary History* 38, no. 3 (2007): 479–504.
Hollier, Denis, and William Rodarmor. "Mimesis and Castration." *October* 31 (1984): 3–15.
Holmes, Anna. "One Thing Is Certain: Right Now, Yale University & Aliza Shvarts '08 Are 100% Annoying." Jezebel.com. http://jezebel.com/381279/one-thing-is-certain-right-now-yale-university--aliza-shvarts-08-are-100-annoying.4/17/08.
Homer, Sean. *Jacques Lacan*. London: Routledge, 2005.
Howarth, Sophie. "Piero Manzoni: Artist's Shit 1961." http://www.tate.org.uk/art/artworks/manzoni-artists-shit-t07667/text-summary.
Hudson, David. "Cannes 2011. Jafar Panahi's 'This Is Not a Film.'" *MUBI*. http://mubi.com/notebook/posts/cannes-2011-jafar-panahis-this-is-not-a-film.
Huffingtonpost. "Aliza Shvarts Insists Miscarriage Art Project Is Real." *Huffpost Health Living*. http://www.huffingtonpost.com/2008/04/17/yale-student-artificially_n_97194.html.
The Joe Schmo Show. Directed by Danny Salles. 2004.
Johnston, Adrian. "The Cynic's Fetish: Slavoj Žižek and the Dynamics of Belief." *Psychoanalysis, Culture, & Society* 9, no. 3 (2004): 259–283.
Kasman, Daniel. "Notebook Review: Jafar Panahi and Mojtaba Mirtahmasb's 'This Is Not a Film.'" February 29, 2012. https://mubi.com/notebook/posts/notebook-reviews-jafar-panahi-and-mojtaba-mirtahmasbs-this-is-not-a-film.
KellyMom Parenting Breastfeeding. http://kellymom.com
Keogh, Tom. Editorial Review. http://www.amazon.com/exec/obidos/tg/detail//B0001XAODO/qid=1111774163/sr=81/ref=pd_csp_1/00243854213729666?v=glance&s=dvd&n=507846.
Kouvaros, George. "'We Do Not Die Twice': Realism and Cinema." *The SAGE Handbook of Film Studies*, 376–391. London: SAGE Publications, 2008.
Kracauer, Siegfried, *Theory of Film: The Redemption of Physical Reality*. Princeton, NJ: Princeton University Press, 1997.
Krips, Henry. *Fetish: An Erotics of Culture*. New York: Cornell University Press, 1999.
Krips, Henry. "A Mass Media Cure for Auschwitz: Adorno, Kafka, and Žižek. *International Journal of Žižek Studies* 1, no. 4 (2007). http://Žižekstudies.org/index.php/ijzs/article/view/67/132.
Kristeva, Julia. *Powers of Horror: An Essay on Abjection*. New York: Columbia University Press, 1982.

Kukla, Rebecca. "Ethics and Ideology in Breastfeeding Advocacy Campaigns." *Hypatia* 21, no. 1 (2006): 157–180.

Lacan, Jacques. *Anxiety: The Seminar of Jacques Lacan, Book X*. Edited by Jacques-Alain Miller. Translated by A. R. Price. Cambridge: Polity, 2014.

Lacan, Jacques. *Ecrits: A Selection*. Translated by Alan Sheridan. New York: Tavistock, 1977.

Lacan, Jacques. *Encore: The Seminar of Jacques Lacan, Book XX*. Edited by Jacques-Alain Miller. Translated by Bruce Fink. New York: Norton, 1999.

Lacan, Jacques. *The Four Fundamental Concepts of Psychoanalysis: The Seminar of Jacques Lacan, Book XI*. Edited by Jacques-Alain Miller. Translated by Alan Sheridan. New York: Norton, 1998.

Laist, Randy. "The Hyperreal Theme in 1990s American Cinema." *Americana: The Journal of American Popular Culture (1990–present)* 9, no. 1 (2010). http://www.americanpopularculture.com/journal/articles/spring_2010/laist.htm.

La Leche League. *The Womanly Art of Breast-feeding*. New York: Plume, 2004.

La Leche League International. http://www.lalecheleague.org/

Lapsley, Robert, and Michael Westlake. *Film Theory: An Introduction*. Manchester: Manchester University Press, 1988.

Lastra, James F. "Why Is This Absurd Picture Here? Ethnology/Heterology/Buñuel." In *Rites of Realism*. Edited by Ivone Margulies, 185–214. Durham, NC: Duke University Press, 2003.

Longworth, Karina. "*This Is Not a Film*: Jafar Panahi Is a Filmmaker Who Isn't." *Phoenix New Times*. http://www.phoenixnewtimes.com/movies/this-is-not-a-film-in-film-nist-6709885.

Lukács, Georg. *Essays on Realism*. Edited by Rodney Livingstone. Translated by David Fernbach. Cambridge, MA: MIT Press, 1981.

MacCabe, Colin. "Realism and the Cinema: Notes on Some Brechtian Theses." *Screen* 15, no. 2 (1974): 7–27.

MacCabe, Colin. Foreword to *In Other Worlds: Essays in Cultural Politics*. Translated by Gayatri Chakravorty Spivak. London: Taylor & Francis, 1987.

MacCabe, Colin. "Riviera Eschatology." *Film Quarterly* 65, no. 1 (2011): 63–65.

Maizels, Neil. "Melancholia, Cosmopolis and Modern Pain." *Arena Magazine*, 2012. http://www.academia.edu/4117527/Melancholia_and_Cosmopolis_Arena_Magazine.

Marguilies, Ivonne. "Bodies Too Much." *Rites of Realism*. Edited by Ivone Margulies. Durham, NC: Duke University Press, 2003.

Massumi, Brian. "*Realer Than Real: The Simulacrum According to Deleuze and Guattari*." http://www.brianmassumi.com/textes/REALERTHANREAL.pdf.

McGowan, Todd. *The Fictional Christopher Nolan*. Austin: University of Texas Press, 2012.

Miller, Jacques-Alain. "The Symptom and the Body Event." Translated by Barbara P. Fulks. *Lacanian Ink* 19 (2001): 4–47.

Milzroff, Rebecca. "Can You Believe This?" *NY Magazine*. http://nymag.com/movies/features/68100/.

Modleski, Tania. *The Women Who Knew Too Much: Hitchcock and Feminist Theory*. New York: Routledge, 1988.

Morrissey, Tracie Egan Morrissey. "*Catfish* Filmmakers Get the Third Degree," http://jezebel.com/5661158/catfish-filmmakers-get-the-third-degree,10/11/10.

Mulvey, Laura. "Visual Pleasures and Narrative Cinema." *Screen* 16, no. 3 (1975): 6–19.

Nichols, Bill. *Representing Reality: Issues and Concepts in Documentary*. Bloomington: Indiana University Press, 1992.
Nicholson, Rebecca. "Could Dark Dating-Show Satire *UnReal* Kill Reality TV?" http://www.theguardian.com/tv-and-radio/tvandradioblog/2015/jul/14/could-dark-dating-show-satire-unreal-kill-reality-tv.
Oakley, Ann. *Fracture: Adventures of a Broken Body*. Bristol: Policy Press, 2007.
Ouellette, Laurie. "'Take Responsibility for Yourself': *Judge Judy* and the Neoliberal Citizen." In *Reality TV: Remaking Television Culture*, edited by Susan Murray and Laurie Ouellette, 231–250. New York: New York University Press, 2004.
Owen, Rob. "Jessica Lynch Movie." http://old.post-gazette.com/tv/20030710owen0710fnp2.asp.
Peterson, Christopher. "The Magic Cave of Allegory: Lars von Trier's *Melancholia*." *Discourse* 35, no. 3 (2013): 400–422.
Pieters, Jürgen, and Kris Pint. *Roland Barthes Retroactively: Reading the Collège de France Lectures Volume 31*, edited by Jürgen Pieters and Kris Pint. Edinburgh: Edinburgh University Press, 2008.
Post-Gazette.com. "'Catfish' Swears It's All True," http://www.post-gazette.com/pg/10274/1091655-60.stm.
Powers, Martine, Zachary Abrahamson, and Thomas Kaplan. "Shvartz, Yale Clash over Project." *Yale Daily News*, April 18, 2008. http://www.yaledailynews.com/news/university-news/2008/04/18/shvarts-yale-clash-over-project/.
Prusi, Renee. "Thrilled to Be Chosen: Pierce Happy to Be Part of Local Art Exhibit." *Miningjournal*. http://www.miningjournal.net/page/content.detail/id/563668/Thrilled-to-be-chosen.html.
Ragland-Sullivan, Ellie. "The Sexual Masquerade: A Lacanian Theory of Sexual Difference." In *Lacan and the Subject of Language*, edited by Ellie Ragland-Sullivan and Mark Bracher, 49–80. New York: Routledge, 1991.
Ralske, Josh. "Review." http://www.allmovie.com/movie/catfish-v507353/review
Rancière, Jacques. *Aesthetics and Its Discontents*. Translated by Steven Corcoran. Cambridge: Polity Press, 2009.
Rancière, Jacques. *The Emancipated Spectator*. Translated by Gregory Elliott. London: Verso, 2009.
Rancière, Jacques. *The Intervals of Cinema*. Translated by John Howe. London: Verso, 2014.
Rancière, Jacques. "Jacques-Rancière Interview 2007." *Void Manufacturing*. http://voidmanufacturing.wordpress.com/2008/10/15/jacques-Rancière-interview-2007.
Rancière, Jacques. *Politics of Aesthetics*. London: Continuum, 2006.
Rectanus, Mark. *Culture Incorporated: Museums, Artists, and Corporate Sponsorships*. Minneapolis: University of Minnesota Press, 2002.
Riskin, Jessica. "The Defecating Duck, Or, The Ambiguous Origins of Artificial Life." *Critical Inquiry* 20, no. 4 (Summer 2003): 599–633.
Rose, Jacqueline. *Sexuality in the Field of Vision*. London: Verso, 1986.
Rosen, Philip. "History of Image, Image of History: Subject and Ontology in Bazin." In *Rites of Realism*, edited by Ivone Margulies, 42–79. Durham, NC: Duke University Press, 2002.
Rosin, Hannah. "The Case Against Breast-Feeding." *The Atlantic*, April 2009. http://www.theatlantic.com.
Safatle, Vladimir. "Mirrors without Images: Mimesis and Recognition in Lacan and Adorno." http://www.oocities.org/vladimirsafatle/vladi089.htm.

Schor, Naomi. *Reading in Detail: Aesthetics and the Feminine*. London: Routledge, 2007.
Scott, A. O. "The World Where You Aren't What You Post." http://www.nytimes.com/2010/09/17/movies/17catfish.html?_r=0.
Shaviro, Steven. "Melancholia or, the Romantic Anti-Sublime." *Sequence* 1, no. 1 (2012): 3–55. http://reframe.sussex.ac.uk/sequence/files/2012/12/MELANCHOLIA-or-The-Romantic-Anti-Sublime-SEQUENCE-1.1-2012-Steven-Shaviro.pdf.
Sobchack, Vivian. *The Address of the Eye: A Phenomenology of Film Experience*. Princeton, NJ: Princeton University Press, 1992.
Solon, Olivia. "Catfish Review and Interview with Nev Schulman." *Wired*, December 10, 2010. http://www.wired.co.uk/news/archive/2010-12/10/catfish-review-and-interview?page=all.
This Is Not a Film. Directed by Jafar Panahi and Mojtaba Mirtahmasb. 2011.
U.S. Department of Health and Human Services. *US Government's 2004 National Breastfeeding Awareness Campaign*. http://www.womenshealth.gov/breastfeeding/?page=Campaign.
Verhaeghe, Paul. *Beyond Gender: From Subject to Drive*. New York: Other Press, 2001.
Womenshealth. "Breastfeeding." http://womenshealth.gov/breastfeeding/breastfeeding-in-public/.
Wright, Elizabeth. *Lacan and Postfeminism*. Cambridge: Icon Books, 2000.
Yaledailynews. "Shvartz, Yale Clash over Project." http://yaledailynews.com/blog/2008/04/18/shwartz-yale-clash-over-project/.
Zalloua, Zaha. "Žižek with French Feminism: Enjoyment and the Feminine Logic of the 'Not-All.'" *Intertexts* 18, no. 2 (2014): 109–130.
Žižek, Slavoj. *Der Ärger mit dem Realen* [Troubles with the Real]. Vienna: Sonderzahl, 2008.
Žižek, Slavoj. "Desire: Drive = Truth: Knowledge." In *Umbr(a)*, edited by Daniel G. Collins, 147–152. Buffalo, NY: The Center for the Study of Psychoanalysis and Culture, 1997.
Žižek, Slavoj. *The Fright of Real Tears: Krzystof Kieslowski Between Theory and Post-Theory*. London: BFI Publishing, 2001.
Žižek, Slavoj. *How to Read Lacan*. New York: Norton, 2007.
Žižek, Slavoj. *Interrogating the Real*. Edited by Rex Butler and Scott Stephens. New York: Continuum, 2005.
Žižek, Slavoj. "Introduction." In *Mapping Ideology*, edited by Slavoj Žižek. London: Verso, 1994.
Žižek, Slavoj. "Melancholia and the Act." *Critical Inquiry* 26, no. 4 (2000), 657–672.
Žižek, Slavoj. *On Belief*. New York, Routledge. 2001.
Žižek, Slavoj. "The Optimism of Melancholia." http:bigthink.com/videos/the-optimism-of-melancholia.
Žižek, Slavoj. *Organs Without Bodies: Deleuze and Consequences*. New York: Routledge, 2004.
Žižek, Slavoj. *Plague of Fantasies*. London: Verso, 1997.
Žižek, Slavoj. *The Sublime Object of Ideology*. London: Verso, 1989.
Žižek, Slavoj. *Tarrying with the Negative: Kant, Hegel, and the Critique of Ideology*. Durham, NC: Duke University Press, 1993.
Žižek, Slavoj. "The Truth Arises from Misrecognition Part 1." In *Lacan and the Subject of Language*, edited by Ellie Ragland-Sullivan and Mark Bracher, 188–212. New York: Routledge, 1991.
Zupančič, Alenka. "Realism in Psychoanalysis." *European Journal of Psychoanalysis* 32 (2011): 29–48.

INDEX

abject, the, 80, 86
aesthetic politics, 2–5, 13, 17–18, 25, 29–30, 32, 34–35, 47, 56, 60–61, 73–74, 126
aesthetic regime, 17, 27, 30–32, 34–40, 47, 93
Allen, Richard, 7
American Family, An, 75
anxiety, 75, 92–96, 99, 102–106, 114–119, 121, 128

Badinter, Elisabeth, 93–94
Barthes, Roland, 125
Bastian, Heiner, 27
Baudrillard, Jean, 48, 77
    deterrence function, 74–75
    illusion vs. virtuality, 9, 11
    simulation, 23–24, 53–55, 126–127
    simulation vs. dissimulation, 11
    trompe l'oeil vs. virtuality, 8, 11
Bazin, André, 41, 44–45, 49–50, 113
belief, 18–20, 22–26, 121–122
Bentham, Jeremy, 81
Bhabha, Homi, 84, 86
Big Brother, 15, 62, 65, 68–69, 73
big Other, 18–23, 82, 101, 111, 113, 121–122, 125
Bishop, Claire, 65
"Bitte liebt Österreich," 15, 59, 61–62, 64, 68, 127
Blum, Linda, M., 101, 103
Bodyworlds, 15, 79–81, 83–84, 128
Bordo, Susan, 21
Bozovic, Miran, 81–82
breastfeeding, 91–108, 128
Brousse, Marie-Hélène, 106

Buchanan, Kyle, 33
Burgin, Victor, 63

Callois, Roger, 81–82
Catfish, 14, 31–37, 40, 42–44, 48–50, 126–127
Cloaca, 15, 79–81, 84, 87–90, 128
Conley, Tom, 49
consciousness-raising, 12–13, 73
Copjec, Joan, 94–95, 99, 103–105
Cowie, Elizabeth, 77
Creed, Barbara, 10, 68–69, 77
cynicism, 23, 123–125

Daly, Glyn, 107
Daney, Serge, 41
Danto, Arthur, 28–29
Delvoye, Wim, 15, 79, 81, 84, 88–90, 128
Digesting Duck, 87–88, 90
disavowal, 86, 99, 102, 118–119, 126
dissensus, 13–14, 32, 34, 61, 108, 129
dissimulation, 5, 7, 11, 14–15, 19, 25–26, 28, 52–55
double deception, 52, 88
doubt, 18–20, 22, 42, 117

Edelman, Lee, 120
Eisler, Judith, 6–7, 9
Elizabeth Smart Story, The, 69–70, 76
Elmo, 1–4, 12
enunciated, 3–5, 42
enunciation, 3–5, 42
epistemological uncertainty, 5, 11, 53, 55, 57
equivocation, 6

feminine masquerade, 68, 76, 111
fetishistic inversion, 68, 72–73
Fink, Bruce, 106, 114
Flight of the Conchords, 24–26
FPÖ, 60
Freud, Sigmund, 84–85, 102, 114, 116–117
Frosch, Jon, 49

Galindo, Pete, 62
Gaspin, Jeff, 70
Greeves, Susana, 19, 27

Haider, Jörg, 60
Hall, Stuart, 64–65
Hansen, Miriam, 50
Hanson, Duane, 19
Harari, Roberto, 85, 87, 105–106
Hausman, Bernice L., 97–98, 100
Headlong, 82–83
heterology, 37–38, 40
Hollier, Denis, 6, 81–82
Homer, Sean, 82
hypervirtuality, 9–10

ideology, 4, 12, 15, 17, 22, 61–62, 67, 71
illusion, 9, 16
imaginary, the, 16, 54–55, 91, 93–94, 96, 100, 102–106, 108, 129

Jenkins, Mark, 28–30, 126
Joe Schmo Show, The, 15, 67–69, 71–76, 128
Joust, Henry, 14, 31, 33–34

Kellner, Douglas, 68
Klasky, Helaine, 51–52
Klein, Melanie, 105
Kontiki, 44
Körperweltern. *See Bodyworlds*
Kouvaros, George, 50
Kracauer, Sigfried, 50
Kristeva, Julia, 80
Kukla, Rebecca, 93, 95

La Leche League International, 15–16, 91, 93, 99–104, 107
Lacan, Jacques, 3, 124, 129
  anxiety, 92, 106, 116–119
  automaton, 113

belief vs. doubt, 19
big Other, 18–20
double deception, 52
drive, 87
ethical act, 120
gaze, 76–77
imaginary, 92, 96, 102
jouissance, 106–107
masquerade, 68, 76, 122
melancholia, 116
metalanguage, 7, 24, 27
mimicry, 81
non-duped err, the, 89, 123, 125
objet petit a, 105, 117, 119
phallus, 21
Real, 14, 31, 37–39, 44–45, 50, 54, 57, 75, 85, 93, 102, 108
reality, 43
reality and fantasy, 24
reality and the Real, 48, 107
repetition, 85
sexuation, 75, 111–112
signifier, 82–83
subject supposed to believe, 25
symbolic, 13, 92, 96, 102, 107–108
trompe l'oeil, 7
truth and deception, 13–14
truth and fiction, 2–3, 61
Vorstellungsrepräsentanz, 26
Zeuxis and Parrhasios, 27
Lanzmann, Claude, 39
Lars and the Real Girl, 20–22, 24–26
Lastra, James F., 6
Levi-Strauss, Claude, 124
Love Soup, 26–29, 42
Luck, Merlin, 69, 73
Lukács, Georg, 60–61

MacCabe, Colin, 12, 64, 115
Maizels, Neil, 114, 119
Manzoni, Piero, 89
Margulies, Ivonne, 41
Massumi, Brian, 7, 54
melancholia, 114–119
Melancholia, 16, 111–122, 129
Merde d'Artista, 89
Merleau-Ponty, Maurice, 83
metalanguage, 3–6, 18, 24, 26–30, 41–42
Milner, Jacques-Alain, 83
Milzoff, Rebecca, 43

[152] *Index*

mimesis, 9, 80–81, 84
mimicry, 80–82, 84, 86
minimal difference, 80, 85–86
Mirtahmasb, Mojtaba, 31, 41, 45, 49
Mueck, Ron, 14, 17–19, 24, 27–30, 126
Mulvey, Laura, 67–68, 76
Modleski, Tania, 68

National Breastfeeding Awareness Campaign (2004), 15–16, 91, 93–94, 96–100, 104
Nichols, Bill, 42–43
non-duped err, the, 89, 123–126, 129
Not an Alternative, 6–7

object petit a, 82, 87, 105, 119
ontological indeterminacy, 5, 8, 11, 23–24, 53, 55, 57
Ouellette, Laurie, 62

Panahi, Jafar, 14, 31, 40–41, 45–49, 127
parody, 68, 74, 77, 128
Peterson, Chris, 113, 115, 121
phallus, 21–23
photorealism, 6–7
"Please Love Austria." *See* "Bitte liebt Österreich"
projective illusion, 8

radical democracy, 59, 65, 128
Rancière, Jacques, 8, 10, 21, 26, 36, 48, 61, 65, 77, 126–127
    aesthetic politics, 2–4, 13–14, 17–18, 29–32, 34–35, 47, 49, 56, 60–61, 73
    aesthetic regime, 17, 31, 35, 37–39, 93, 108
    democracy, 60
    dissensus, 14, 129
    heterology, 37
    representative regime, 17, 93, 109
    sensible, the, 14, 37
    unrepresentable, the, 38–39
Reagans, The, 69–71, 76
Real, the, 14, 16, 25, 31, 37–40, 43–45, 47–50, 54–55, 57, 75–76, 85–86, 89, 91, 93–95, 98–99, 102–105, 107–108, 117, 120–122, 124, 127–129
Real-ism, 14, 31, 50

realist illusion, 2, 6, 29
Rectanus, Mark, 63
repetition, 85–86
representative regime, 14, 17, 21, 27, 29, 31–32, 34–39, 47, 93, 126
return, 85
Rose, Jacqueline, 75
Rosen, Philip, 44
Rosin, Hanna, 91–93, 101, 107–108, 129

Saussure, Ferdinand, de, 84
Saving Jessica Lynch, 69–70, 76
Schlingensief, Christoph, 15, 59–62, 64–65, 68, 127–128
Schor, Naomi, 9, 19, 28–29
Schulman, Ariel (Rev), 14, 31, 33–34, 43
Schulman, Yaniv (Nev), 31, 33–37, 42–44
Scott, A. O., 126
Seinfeld, 82
sensible, the, 3, 8, 13–14, 18, 30, 32, 34–37, 40, 49–50, 56, 60, 74
sexuation, 75, 111–112
Shaviro, Steven, 112, 120
Shoah, 39
Shvarts, Aliza, 14, 51–53, 55–56, 127
simulacrum, 6–7, 11, 54, 84, 126
simulation, 11, 14–15, 23–24, 48, 52–55, 88, 90, 126–127
Sobchack, Vivian, 83
Spivak, Gayatri, 64
Spurlock, Morgan, 42
subject supposed to believe, 20, 22, 25–26, 122
symbolic, the, 13–14, 16, 37–39, 48, 50, 54–55, 57, 76, 82, 85–86, 91, 93–96, 100, 102, 104–108, 112, 116, 122–125, 127, 129

This is Not a Film, 14, 31, 40–42, 45–50, 126–127
Toohey's, 2–4
trompe l'oeil, 7–10, 18–19, 27–29, 72

UnREAL, 74–75
unrepresentable, the, 37–40, 47

Vaucanson, Jacques, 87–88, 90
Verhaeghe, Paul, 54, 108
verisimilitude, 6, 9, 28, 84, 88
virtual reality, 10–11

virtuality, 8–9, 11
Von Hagens, Gunther, 15, 79–80, 128
Von Trier, Lars, 16, 111–114, 119, 129
Vorstelungsrepräsentanz, 26

Zalloua, Zahi, 120
Žižek, Slavoj, 32, 48, 53, 60, 63, 77, 86, 96, 101, 122–125
  belief, 19–20, 23, 122
  big Other, 20–22
  drive, 87

ideology, 4, 12, 22, 61, 71
lie in the form of truth, 27
on *Melancholia*, 111, 113–114, 119, 122
melancholics, 116
metalanguage, 3
overconforming, 45, 95
parody, 71, 73
Real, 38
trauma, 114
truth in the form of a lie, 27, 45, 52, 61

www.ingramcontent.com/pod-product-compliance
Lightning Source LLC
Chambersburg PA
CBHW062008200625
28498CB00021B/472